Michael Thomas
Poetry 7

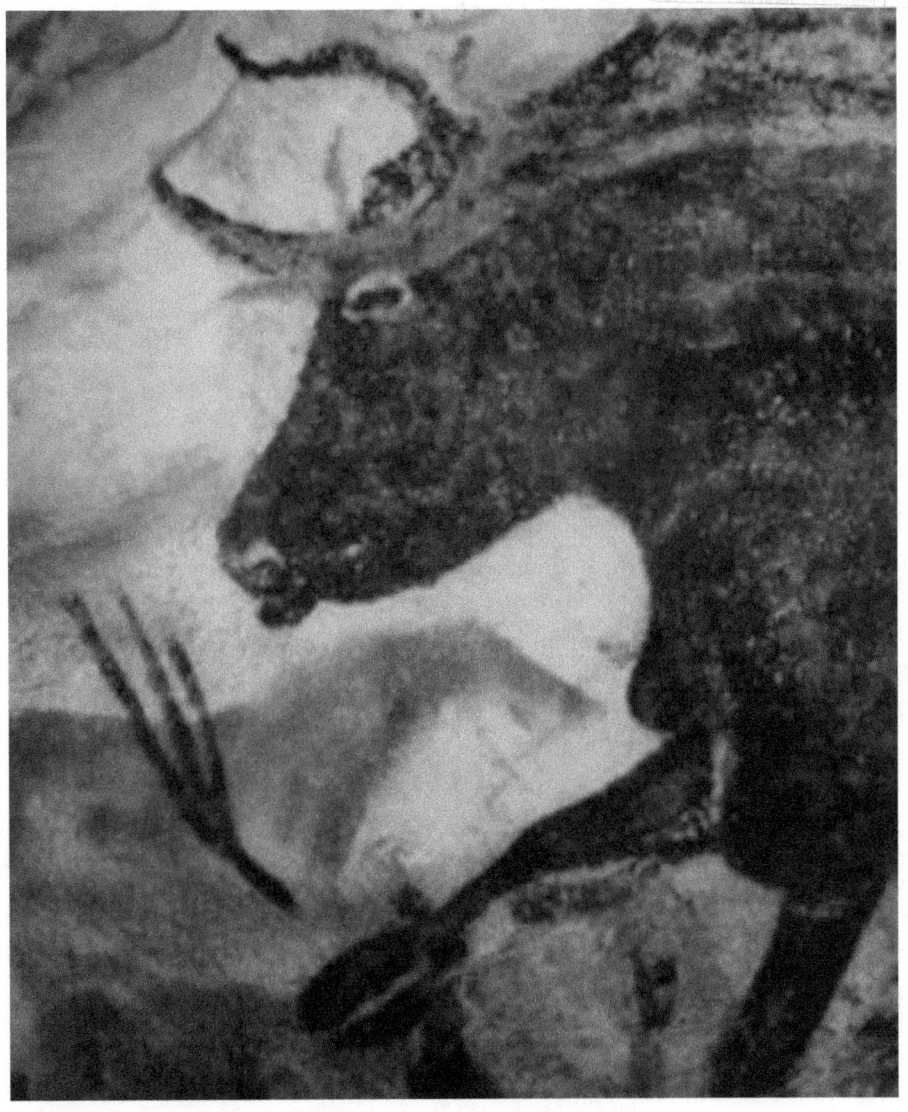

Michael Thomas
Poetry 7

Paperback
ISBN: 978-1-943974-13-9
Library of Congress Controll Number: 2017937892

Published by: Shoestring Book Publishing

Copyright 2017
By, Michael Thomas

All rights reserved.
Printed in the Unites States of America

No part of this book may be reproduced, stored in a Retrieval system, or transmitted in any form, Electronic, mechanical; or by other means whatsoever, Without written permission from the author, Except for The case of brief quotations within reviews and critical Articles

Layout and design by Shoestring Book Publishing

For information address:
Shoestringpublishing4u@gmail.com
www.shoestringbookpublishing.com

Michael Thomas Poetry 7

By Michael Thomas

Shoestring Book Publishing

Acknowledgements

This book is dedicated to my publishers, Alison & Allan Emery of Shoestring Book Publishing, who exceed the boundaries of protocol by being my mentors, advisors, friends and ultimately the best publishers I could have ever expected to find.

To trust someone who understands words and their power, is to lay the sword down and accept that which is greater by far. My thanks to both of you, Allan and Alison.

Table of Contents

Being the Rain 1

Comparison 2

My Simplicity 4

Doors 5

Speak of Knives 6

Ineptitude Of Irrelevance 7

Chalice of Love 8

My Redundant Bird 10

Rays of Light 11

Sandy is Dandy / Liquor is Quicker 12

For The Thin Line Of Fame Dissolving 14

Time 15

Shelly and Jim 16

An Earth Heaven 17

What Am I To Love? 18

Reach a Safe Place 19

The Ones I Cannot See 20

Tomorrow 21

Pain 22

Cold Mountain Snippets 24

Trust 25

Barbara 26

Stones in Water 27

Moonbeams 28

Vines 29

A Haven 30

Reach a Safe Place 32

Resolution of Poetry 34

Life Ends So It Begins 35

Giving Up 36

Love's Melody 37

Invictus de mortis – Unconquered Of Death 38

Days of Days 39

Love Inside Us 40

Sorrow 41

Is there anybody out there 42

Clarity Of Prayer 44

Nocturne To Love 45

For Our Children 46

Lips That Broke The Solemn Morn 47

Silted Sandy Bottomless Silence 48

By Death Shall I Conquer – Per Mortem Vicero 49

In Some Frond Resting Place 50

Rhyming Has Gone Astray 51

Praying To The Gods Keeping My Bases Covered 52

The Rich 53

A Requiem For The Non-Dead 54

A Requiem For The Non-Dead Part 2 55

Our Burnt Edges 56

Alone But Never Lonely 57

Ancient Memories 58

Footprints 59

Find You Forever 60

Papa and the Moon 61

Unending Measure 62

Red Inside Our Tenuous Lives 64

Jesus And The Blues 65

What Was Here 66

The Forests of Yesterday 67

Everything New 68

Through A Silent Moment He Whispered To Me 69

Starting All Over 70

It's Only a Miracle 71

War 72

Your Smile a Salvation 74

Being so Mean 76

Vastness 77

Awakening to Hope 78

Our Gentle Hearts Throb With Praying 79

Blood Test 80

In Fondling Youth Allays Time to Spare 81

The Rabbi Prays 82

Displacement 84

Two Minute Warning - Fourth And Goal 85

Fire Of My Soul 86

File Me Away 87

Waiting 88

River Eyes 89

Beatitude Of Mercy 90

We Were 91

Precious Memories 92

You, Three Times Love 94

My Success Becomes My Failure 95

10-Deadliest-Wars-in-Human-History 96

Light That Has Survived 97

The Cat Without A Christmas 98

I Wanna Be With You 99

Heaven 100

Ancient Lore 101

New Year's Poem 102

A Chant Poem 103

I wonder 104

I wonder Aloud 105

Life 106

Being Reborn 107

Forsaken 108

The Peacemakers 109

Comfort of Ancient Times 110

Poems Modeled After 111

Muso Soseki 1275 to 1351 111

Religions 111

Self-Perception 111

A Poem of Nocturne 112

She Who Died Little Known 112

A Poem of Redemption 112

Love By Any Other Name is Lust 113

God's Blessedness 114

The Word 115

Why Do We Need Poetry? 116

It is Last Call 118

My Entry 119

Jabber 120

Latest Poetry Books of Interest 121

Poem Of Emotion 122

A Short Snippet Of My Father,

Mike Ferris Michael Thomas 123

An Essay On Death by Michael Thomas 124

Waiting 126

Note to a Fellow Poet 127

God Who Saw God Inside Himself 128

My Prayer 129

Friday Night 130

A Soul Embedded Night 132

Floating 133

Morning/Evening Dove – Sing Thy Ancient Days 134

In Fortunes Fame 136

To Her 137

I am Happy With Myself 138

"Something" 140

A Short Story 142

Bigger and Better 144

When Everything is Balanced 146

Money Blues 147

Travelling 148

Happy Spring/Easter 149

Letter to Adam 150

Parts of Me 152

The Horse Snorts 153

Hope 154

Tears 155

Oceans Erase Me 156

Women versus Men (Tiresias) 158

Jesus Laughs 160

Life 161

Visiting Gerhard & Martha Woltemade's Grave 162

Autumn Days 163

Leaving You 164

Death 165

My Big Fat Tax Cake 166

Overcoming 168

With You Beside Me 169

Loving my Neighbor 170

Holes in my Head 171

Light Years Ago 172

No Light 173

Today, Ya Finest Lite 174

Reflection 175

With You 176

Silence 177

Just Because 178

Existence as we Know It 180

A Few Friends 182

Women 183

Unselfish Stories 184

Prioritizing of our Information Age 186

The Beast of Degeneracy 190

Various Poems New 191

#1 191

#2 192

#3 193

#4 Lust - A Sonnet 194

#5 195

#6 196

#7 197

#8 198

#9 199

#10 200

Days of Light 201

An Unfulfilled Dream 202

Schubert Lieder Auf dem Wasser Zu Singen, D. 774 – Elly Ameling & Rudolf Jansen 204

Glen Campbell 205

My Ex Wife 206

Round and Round 208

Refrain from the Dance 209

Achilles Awakens 210

My Indiscretions 212

Hope 214

My Daughter 215

Memorial Day Expose 216

Sega Boom 220

Smooth Edge of a Saw 221

Why Wednesday? 222

I am Nothing but Glorified in Magnificence 224

Being the Rain

fill paper bags with me
float your lanterns down my mysterious rivers
there is a forever to my flow
going to or from my ocean family
hail Poseidon in hoary sprays of operas
before the night leaves,
watch the moon slice me in two
let the roar of undiminished waves collect
upon roiled
sandy beaches
and then cover us together
 with the quiet patter of silence

Comparison

seven years recovering from her
upshot is that she was never the right person
for a long term relationship
she was a short term lover with a short fuse and explosive sex
question is: what good is sex when you are alone years later

it has been over forty years
I encountered her on face book and learned this:
she is a person who takes

in between her and now,
I have had forty years of giving to one woman
in the process I have learned to give to all the people around me

my forty year friend died
and I am so proud to have loved her
love, to me, is learning to give without asking anything back
 my reward is peace
my reward is a comfortable life with money
and acknowledgement
I am proud to have eleven books at Amazon
with more in the works

encountering my old lover on face book was as disappointing
   as knowing her forty years ago
she never asked me how I was doing
she only talked about how she was doing
after her self-centered discussion, she left
   without even a word of praise for my books

fact is, I know myself and now,
do not need her praise
all the people in my world, at present,
are kind loving people

they exchange good things with me

let me tell you about connecting with old lovers
It proves to be a springboard for the future
and with her I was a selfish man interested only in sex
without her for forty years
I have learned how inconsequential sex is
   in place of love for others

old lovers are the experience needed for new love
to spring forth from
so, thank you old lovers because without you
I would have nothing to

   compare too

My Simplicity

begun infantile
post embryonic
"sublime"
conceived pure

first being sublimity as awareness of heaven in simplicity
that movement outside of our plane as the earth's path
or the stars diverging to oblique emptiness
is who I am within my vacuity of indicative differences

next, the potentiality to succeed inherent within action
there never is any doubt as to attainment of goals
no self-deprecation ever takes hold long enough
to deter the arrow shot of aim toward completion

third is the power to further
like the pyramids, stone-by-stone
like the washing of ocean waves
turning stone into beach sand
moving each increment above itself
in a "Feng Shui" of well-placed order

last is my indefatigable perseverance
I never stop to delay
I move steamroller to completion
sleeping or rest comes after finishing

within the four stages of sublime, success, furthering
and sticktoitiveness

I maintain my balance against all odds
and even prepare myself for death
with these four qualities of personality that are Zen-like
or just simple rules

Doors

distances defy drama
as short as the life of an apple

hit ball against wall
no need to worry if you fall
earth will rise up perpendicular

we all bend to the brittle branch
when even our stiff pride pushes us along

more than knowledge is the curl of our cursing
as we turn tails on established thoughts
 and dive into darkness

I have been the hawk
been the sequential moon path over silent tree lines
before the mongoose or the quaint loon bestirred by lily pads

oh how winter takes us into its coiled curlicues
breaks us as crystal icicles shattered by frost

but, worry not,
for life continues through the veil
what is now-here is now-there
as doors opened to infinity close tomorrow

Speak of Knives

speak of blood
aprons of slaughter
meat store butcher
gentle man who wields a knife with assurance

see the vacuous look in his eyes
he cannot speak of things intimate
there is a wall over which he will never climb

speak of the innocence of cutting into life
with no thought of souls, after or before life

we can only love the person who gave us life
through his silence

Ineptitude Of Irrelevance

They come from the world of, "I told you so's"
a world void of pulchritude
where the promise of minutiae
fills the space to exhaustion

I exhale
inhale the air of sacredness

I see
but wait for colors to change
never - Oh! spare me the charcoal

this world of black and white
pushes rainbows into corners
builds upon chiaroscuro in grays
muted silhouettes of sadness

I am heavy for blue visions
left over prisms of promise

I do not want to be drawn into the void
I resist the dark hole intake

how can I out-wait the emptiness
be patient with valueless words
missing the points of plentitude
I will become the Buddha of bananas

Chalice of Love

soft are the memories of love
placed within the chalice of our hearts
hidden in our holy-of-holy's
kept safe from negative interpretations

we venture into love
our lovers have their memories
we cannot take responsibility for their dreams

across the span of our lives
we build bits of songs within our souls

like gypsy romance
we keep to ourselves the rendering of happiness
when we open the sacred places within us
the spirit of light bathes us with its white healing
and keeps us safe in the chambers of blessedness Listening

In annals of jazz groups, improvisation reigns supreme.
The extemporaneous off-the-cuff riffs or sustained melodies
that run through the piece of music,
are what we listen for as pleasing.

It is a common rule,
that good jazz musicians practice their scales
often using Bach as the basis for their collected memorized pieces.
The most important aspect of rounding out a song,
is how the sections tie into each other.

I love how Keith Jarrett puts his sections of sound together.
He will do what good musicians do, and that is:
develop sounds so that circles of keys or chord changes fit
into a new way of hearing what he is trying to create.

Jimmy Hendricks laced his music with guitar sounds that were
so fresh to our ears, even fresher today when we listen to him.

Some of my favorite musicians make my ears perk up
with their unified chord changes.
One of my absolute best writers are classical like

Mozart, Beethoven or Brahms,
but players like Robert Plant or Emerson,
Lake & Palmer, can be listened to as if their work
is classical in scope.

Yellowjackets are a group who exemplify developmental jazz
and they make each song different with their
adaptations of fresh melodies.

All this is good, but how the sounds affect us is what is important.
I remember once hiking into the mountains near Denver when,
coming to an outlook so all-encompassing in its depth of view,
that a sign posted by the rangers said: "This is the mountain.
It is here always, tell us what you see that is different."

I hear boundless sounds slipping off the ends of my hearing.

Where notes chase each other into echoes
lapping over and under.
I hear the silence of spiritual awakening
rising out of the mistiness of
drums, steel guitar, piano, saxophone or violin
collecting themselves as if talking together coherently.

I hear my heart healing itself with the bands
of ballads or choral ministrations.
I let those parts of me that lie sleeping,
become awoken refreshed.
I become the words and lyrics
as if appendages within my soul.

It is me as one-with-the-music.
It is all so adaptable to some inner magic of love.

Michael Thomas

My Redundant Bird

Funny thing birds sing
to complain about pollution.
The sound of car engines
incessant stream of expressways
makes their head dead to rare silences.
Birds sing to make us aware
of the stillness surrounding seasons.

My favorite paradoxical bird is the Kingfisher
because they holler when they dive to catch a fish.
I mean, how audacious to warn the fish to "look-out".

The greatest dichotomy is the swift winged birds
that ride the currents with the lift of temperature shifts.
They bespeak of death in the quietness of their plunging for prey.
The little Nuthatch ain't a bird. It is a nervous little cutie.
It walks up and down trees so fast as it eats insects.

The Robin makes merry with a worm in its mouth.
Talk about being hungry, well there goes the worm
into the extended mouths of its chitty-chat children in the nest.
This parent gives up food to keep its young fed.

Fool the best of them is the buffalo bird or cow bird that
lays its eggs in the nests of other birds. Migrant wanderers
tend to look for ways to propagate and the cow bird is shameless.
My favorite bird is my ex-wife. She never stops complaining
of me divorcing her and so I call her the redundant bird.

Rays of Light

The beleaguered heart
is the heart of caution.

The confident heart
is the heart of venturesome.

We cannot be free of self-indulgence
until we free ourselves from our self-pity.

Color my memories in blood roses
laid upon the bier of my timelessness.

How often we return to the colors of joy
is how we color our remembrances.

Mellow is my soul
from having been
pricked by the rose
of love.

Into my dreams of her are forty years of happiness
buried beneath the trellis of sanguine mysteries.
Let this flower speak of love's nourishment
fed by the sun of secrets
quieted by the moon of blue.

Love is entwined with the seasons
as flowers follow the days of light.

Sandy is Dandy / Liquor is Quicker

She's got a hot eye for cold-cut-poetry.
Sandy the semper fidelis heart so true.

Way above the clouds, the angels sleep.
Deep in the center of time where not clock ticks,
she is the high and the core of angelic simplicity.

If you put Jesus in a bottle and throw it into the ocean,
she will fish it out for you and release our Lord, who
will grant you three wishes: one for the money,
two for the show, three for the little people who
fill the night forest with merriment and song.

Take all of her poems and put them into a prayer book.
You will get a rhyming collection of loveliness.

She sends Hallmark out to find better writers.
She makes sounds with her polished endings.

Sandy says: "Give me your poor and huddled masses,
              I will free them from all their hard tasks"

Sandy is the writer of epistles.
She is the blessed one of words.
She leaves us feeling grateful
by her tell-tale heart.

She does not need a monument
or more than a few loose minutes
to kick out the poems of her wishes.

I always feel protected by her ideas.

Now, here is the way to remember Sandy:
Sandy is dandy
Liquor is quicker

For The Thin Line Of Fame Dissolving

Beside a serene temperament I slip into obscurity
Like the literal finale of a whispered mention.
If ever there was a family, I drove them away
Becoming merged within myself illicitly.

Tried by Anubis: Covered in indigo Christ:
Somnolent by Buddha chant: I glide after,
Being singular as "One-With-Instantcy"

Ahhh! Do not give time its demands.
There are no excuses for gallantry,
Love was neither "here-nor-there" and
Neighborly-ness coveted a black moon.

Gathered up skirt-like over ocean spans,
See a shadowed Cyclops one-eyed dancing,
Implacable ballet pirouetted-prancing gait
And bow to darkness along a blue silence.

I was always in control
But never self-assured
Like a Luna Moth
To Yesterday.

Time

I have been travelling this road
Looking for the end of it.
Road of broken trees spending their branches
Thick on the ground.
I have been slow to find the easy way
To get around this dream
of a journey through time
That fails to stop the anger deep in me.

I spent all my light inside darkness of ages.
I surrendered all my innocence in rages.
Look into the rear view mirror outrunning the wind.
See the sky hiding the end of the highway of my life.
I am burdened by faces forgetting kindness.
My heart is sore from acts of the ungenerous.
Call feathers of angels to fall over me in grace.
Sweep me away in mists covering my eyes.

I have been on a journey of my collected pain
from ten thousand friendless miles of changes.

Cover me over with reasons for a godless sign.
Hide me below the earth of natural causes.
I am brother to the arms of redemption.
I am kin to suspended sweetness of stone.
I am your conscious within my soul.
Look at the heavens falling into pieces before us.
I have been travelling this road
Looking for you at the end of it.

Michael Thomas

Shelly and Jim

Shelly danced
Jim sat
Missionary / He her mission
Sweet fragrant youth
Intangible flower
When we were beautiful
Our life was less than full but overflowing

An Earth Heaven

Soft branched swinging tree shadows
A loft of stars telling stories of distance
Poets of moon highways passing words
A new color blackened to blue prayers
Sits between dry ghosts of eternities

I cannot take in all that the silence has to give out
As my thoughts crawl between melancholic spaces
Delicate sleeping forest flowers rest in their fragrances

I wink and all things disappear
Leaving me embedded in a mystery

All lovers remember their times
All simple smiles emerge from galaxies
This journey leaves sign-posts of peace

There are gods unseen by scented winds
All time is at rest in a tableau of earth's heaven

Michael Thomas

What Am I To Love?

Too many promises creep over dark horizons.
Far too many gardens of brown leafless trees.
She sang a siren hollow tourniquet noose song.
Her lips curdled cider vinegar bitter kissing.

I, the fool, to her, a broken winged sharp-shin bird
she kept caged by love in expectant conditions.

Can you imagine slow acting poison?
A descent into misery with escape impossible.

Pull the walls down. Let the water fall over cheek
and pillow soaked night of sorrow.

What was I to her but an emptiness taken in small doses
caught in between my fantasy and her reality ..

What am I to love but a pilgrim of regret?
What is love when love is not enough?
Tear the eyes out of our head.
Shut our mouth to never speak
Nor decree ourselves happy.

Reach a Safe Place

i. On the overgrown trellis down the walkway, I see the wisp of butterflies upon star-jasmine in the month of June or July; summer bees returning. I watch a large cat stalking reddish fledglings by my yellow-picket fence worn from age, paint flaking away on this hottish day. I am filled.

ii. Ordinary life strikes me easy. Swallows carom in the wind, I truly mean; dodging, fleeting, the burnt sun in witness of corridor's time ... dots of houses lined in rows for cause, who am I but a believer chewing on blade of grass. A spotted dog with floppy ears yaps at children's shiny spinning wheels, a woman hangs white-washed sheets ... breezy breeze to dry and refresh. The neighborhood alive. I was thinking.

iii. Things are easy. I ask what life means when I squeeze lemons into ginger-tea where ice cools this dusty throat, I hear a jingle ... and ice cream truck coming down the road. I've had moments like this writing poems with everything I know; people, apples, streets and trees, looking at stonewalls ants
can sense every moment ...
I watch them closely seeing where they will go.
The world astonishes me.

iv. Contemplation I love you sweetly. I will accompany you down from foothills, tell myself clouds are pillows, making up such strange-odd fellows arriving in the deep sublime of sky.
There's a kite in sight which does a dance;
that it does according to its nature expecting me to cope with it,
I tag along gripping my fingers around its tail,
onto its bridle as though it had chosen me
knowing the wind will take us freely.
Equally as easy. Summer spoke to me.

Michael Thomas

The Ones I Cannot See

the ones I cannot see lie beneath wind-blown leaf
under whisper-collected clouds keeping secrets

birds branched nervous, for ghosts, cry

the many. who have spoken, speak not
in breezes lifting their memories aloft

those awaiting resurrection, sleep
content with arm-crossed-bones`

the ones who cannot see me above dust covered earth
are still as I pass their insignificance buried in dreams

the ones that we avoided yesterday, stay unmoved
beneath the flowers fading, tree-dropping branches

give them prayers to sing them back to death
where their hearts no longer feel life's fears

I have cried no more for their sadness
I have reached the end to their stories
I am freed by grace of angels forever

Tomorrow

sliding shim-sham slipping chute-like
lazy looping gait kicking back strike
hoopla-hoop I let loose stringing on
portals of protrusions obbligato don

I am jiggling by a rhythmic tom-tom
adorable and jaunty as a bom-bom
but my eyes unfocused in a haze
and my soul awakened in a blaze

there are slip-shod contra-dance
feet overlapping reindeer prance
my seismic portals open chakra
catching each moment lock jaw

tear apart lexicon introduce ha
tomorrow will be new blah blah

Michael Thomas

Pain

There was a time of relief
short, though it was, it was
like a needle when the pain
receded, creature like,
inside walls within me.

Outwardly expressionless
masked inwardly chaos
as measures of cinching
severity wrapped itself
against stomach or
concave chest pressure
making breathing
near impossible
as well as sensitivity
so extreme that even
slight touches sent
shooting agony
throughout my
imprisoned cavities.

I remember wishing
so hard for death to find me
that I would have paid
any ransom demanded.

To relay to you, how
my mind blinked
would take more
than I could give
against bundles of
throbbing pounding
incessant drumming.

No space was left for
peace or comfort through
thin layers of my delirium.
Time was spent in yearning
for time to cease and my eyes
close once-and-for-all.
The beleaguered heart
is the heart of caution.

The confident heart
is the heart of venturesome.
 We cannot be free of self-indulgence
until we free ourselves from our self-pity.
 Color my memories in blood roses
laid upon the bier of my timelessness.
 How often we return to the colors of joy
is how we color our remembrances.
 Mellow is my soul
from having been
pricked by the rose
of love.

Into my dreams of her are forty years of happiness
buried beneath the trellis of sanguine mysteries.
Let this flower speak of love's nourishment
fed by the sun of secrets
quieted by the moon of blue.
Love is entwined with the seasons
as flowers follow the days of light.

Cold Mountain Snippets

Today seemed like yesterday.
Birds rang up.
Wind suspended itself.
Love raised or beat me down.
But, it was my hunger won over
and I made a casserole out of all the above and feasted.

She is in my thoughts before breathing.
I try to push her away deeper into her grave,
but up she pops like a lesson I have yet to learn.

Before the "Angel-us" rang across the approaching night
my neighbors cart marked his path from his fields to his barns.
I readied my candle for reading and loosened the binding
on my gown to feel the smooth relaxing of the world inside me
like an elixir narcotic.

This has not been a remarkable day. The cameo fizzed out.
I dried up in the sun and lay upon the grass awaiting the dew.
From one end of the duration till I fall asleep, I will affirm nothing
but the advantage I have over yesterday to be alive for this short time.

Trust

I do not know what death is like
I am sure there is a journey
not dangerous, much like a hike,
into a rainbow that is turning
across a path protected by
angels who watch over me.

I have never seen a god or angel.
The presence of these spirits
can only be felt within our hearts,
so, I let it be as it is, by faith.

But faith alone is not enough
to walk toward an unknown.
It takes a whole lot of water
when you're thirsty, or candy bars
to replenish the weary traveler.

So, I hope God understands the reality
of things needed to welcome the tired.
I am sure that concessions will be there
and the cost will only be a few smiles and trust.

Michael Thomas

Barbara

I understand the meaning of indifference
to your lack of kindness or show of pretense
as whatever you have to say agrees or makes sense
and, in the end, I always walk away secretly saying to myself,
"how dense,
to be her would be to be less than innocence
as a soul empty with no penance -
ghost with no repentance."

"Namaste!" She throws her hair back
like gossamer silk softly winded.
I want her between lessons of love's blindness
as she bends to whisper to me, this prayer:
"Make friends with death while you're alive."
How can I counter her allurement,
she is cupcakes in color.

Before we go too far, remember: There is no heaven.
Don't forget it. It will leave you breathless
to see the dark alleys,
other side of the veil.

Namaste, I always considered it an Indian word,
American, like she said it from South Dakota:
"My Lakota blood boils for you."

That put me to sleep laughing many a night
and I always ended saying "God bless and Namaste."

Stones in Water

Stones in water.
Eyes luminescent from tears
sit at bottomless sorrow
like heaviness in fluid thoughts.

How clear it is to see a sun-stream
when love is less than love in our hearts.

It is so sad: love on the rocks.
We lie hidden in our grief as life pours itself around us.
We never dissolve, because our spirit is greater than love.
We are solid in survival.
We are like agate or chiseled marble within love's memory.

Calling to the future, lovers awaken like rivers flowing.
Calling to the old-stones of yesterday, we lie waiting.

Here is love in its glory, transforming solids to serenades.
Breaking all the rules of caution, love sings open the waters.
Becoming as touch and silver spaces, love washes over us
until it is spent and becomes hard-to-heart
 to wait for tomorrow.

Michael Thomas

Moonbeams

The night is alluring, mysterious, dark,
the moon's edge against black canvas is stark.
Nature's paintbrush has painted the sky,
to night's blanket I yield, breathing a sigh

Nestling in softest velvety black, I sleep,
stars hear my wishes, my secrets they keep.
Earth is illuminated with prisms of light...
a magical, glorious wonder of night

Moonbeams dance, shadows abound,
a night melody plays - silence its sound
I rest on a moonbeam, catch shooting stars
infinity a conundrum, its secrets not ours

Under moon and stars lovers embrace,
they kiss, gaze upwards to see the moon's face,
a face that displays the widest of smiles...
smiles on their love, to bewitch and beguile

Vines

I believe in an invisible spirit. I will call it "All-God"
because it embodies humanity
conjuring each civilization's redemption.

To the earth, I pay homage,
in this writing, to the Morning Glory,
Trumpet Flower, Clematis –
To the grape vines that bind centuries of vineyards
into a history of shaded arbors,
spilling their fruit into the mouths of wine connoisseurs
and tipsy peasants.

I admire these plants clinging to trellises,
fence-lines, apertures creating shade from the sun god
and shadow from the moon magician.

To the sailors adventuring seas.
To the merchants harboring their boats
and venturing inland to sleep beneath swaying trees
where the deer lay the grasses flat from their rest.

To the building of towns and cities with genetic mixtures
of haphazard mating and matching.

To your families bred in homogeneous mitochondria
from the sweat of passion hatching out of the heads
of babies born between the legs of enduring mothers.

I thank the All-God every moment of my existence
for the green plant connections holding us together in love.

Michael Thomas

A Haven

1) From the maelstrom of everyday
in a private fenced garden
on a partially shaded bench
cleaned of bird droppings
dried of a hanging mist:
Here I fail to think
but let emptiness
invade my senses
as time fades
and voices
of angels
speak

2) Have you measured space
between sun's horizon?
Between a moon's shadow
left to dissolve off of
my folded fingers
resting on my knees?
Where am I to escape
these bounds of breath
no longer needing air.
Why do I not cry from joy
of a cricket lacing
edges of solitude
invisible to eyes
closed, meditating.

3) It is a collage of love
parades to memories
of flesh and fantasy.
Let excitement draw
itself in circles over
innocence of desire.

How cooled feverishness
became dull sleep
enclosed hiatus of arms.
I could not discern names,
only eyes of lovers piercing
a darkness of mysteries.
I welcome them with
such gladness.

4) If we are what we perceive,
then each mirror of my relationships
is a turning around of images.
I am all of what I have done.
I am all of what was done to me.
I speak: "Make me one with everything"
Collect me within myself and erase all words.

Oh! Love-sweet-love. Come take me to you.
I am a pilgrim of innocence,
patient to be led into safety.
Into a haven of forgetting.

Reach a Safe Place

i. On the overgrown trellis down the walkway,
I see the butterflies-wisp upon star-jasmine in the month of June
or July; summer bees returning. I watch a large cat stalking reddish
fledglings by my yellow-picket fence worn from age,
paint flaking away on this hottish day. I am filled.

ii. Ordinary life strikes me easy. Swallows carom in the wind,
I truly mean; dodging,
fleeting, the burnt sun in witness of corridor's time..
dots of houses lined in rows for cause,
who am I but a believer chewing on blade of grass.
A spotted dog with floppy ears
yaps at children's shiny-spinning wheels,
a woman hangs white-washed sheets ...
breezy breeze to dry and refresh.
The neighborhood's alive. I was thinking.

iii. Things are easy.
I ask what life means
when I squeeze lemons into ginger-tea
where ice cools this dusty throat, I hear a jingle ...
an ice cream truck coming down the road.
I've had moments like this
writing poems with everything I know;
people, apples, streets and trees,
looking at stonewalls ants can sense every moment ...
I watch them closely seeing where they will go.
The world astonishes me.

iv. Contemplation I love you sweetly.
I will accompany you down from foothills,
tell myself clouds are pillows,
making up such strange-odd fellows arriving
in the deep-sublime sky.
There's a kite in sight which does a dance;
that it does according to its nature.
Expecting me to cope with it,
I tag along, gripping my fingers around its tail,
onto its bridle as though it had chosen me,
knowing the wind will take us freely.
Equally as easy. Summer spoke to me.

Michael Thomas

Resolution of Poetry

Let it be me emerging beneath the melting snow
with a poem that wakes the flowers up to grow.

The balm of spring breeze with sweet pollen
making noses tweak.

If you are reminded of elation
or taken out of rotation
out of line or time
by words of love
then I have
done my
best.

Let the light be brighter
the night much deeper
the heart so lighter
and my spirit rise
to heights higher.

I can only look past the veil of knowing
what signs of significance point us into a dream
where heaviness sheds itself with the flutter of a leaf
and all the old injustices become resolved by indifference.

Life Ends So It Begins

Tomorrow will forget today,
Minds will never borrow
Words old, sans memory,
Stripped clean of sorrow.

Labor on for gratitude
Accepting small parts,
Of fame's cold attitude
Sparrowed in our hearts.

Richness measured by
Poorest of our dreams
Builds itself a mystery
Obscure of all means.

Love is a bugaboo
Betraying all truth.
Feelings a big to-do
Time fades, forsooth.

Give us our penance.
Forgive all our sins.
We must never wince,
Life ends so it begins.

Giving Up

Trying hard to remember all I forgot
Loving less and leaving all I ain't got
Lasting longer than bargained for
I am drinking up all the fine liquor
Thirsty for a sign from the big wide
Got no place on earth to stay or hide

Gather me into a net like fish
Take me to do what you wish
My mother has left me to snow
Where the cold whispers all go

Gentle winds blow me with fury
Little clouds cover me in a hurry
I am a patron of artificial fantasies
Sad victim of silent swirling furies

God take this life away from me
I got no place where I want to be
I need some rest from all the fray
Giving up is all that's left today

Love's Melody

Danger in a voice
Not like hollow terror
Silencing forests abuzz with life.

Humans hardly listen to timber
As innocence of vocal patterns denotes guise.

When we hear lyricism, we are unarmed
Ready to exchange ideas.

It is a grating humdrum sound that sets us armed
To watch for devious behavior and chicanery.

The heart comes out in the sing-song loveliness,
Sweet music lilts itself with words that dance into our ears.

Psychology-of-sound is what puts the child asleep.
Gentle murmuring cuddled into warm arms of the mother.

A lullaby of innocence suspends us in infancy
And keeps us free of evil when we listen to love's melody.

Invictus de mortis –
Unconquered Of Death

Invictus de mortis
Unconquered Of Death
Tamped into terra firma
My eternal soul bit-by-bit
Dissolved by fire, rain, sun
Dust of centuries granulated
Instilled with memories grand
Of all endurance overcome by joy
Reestablished into my thoughts now

We are compendiums of solace
In our silences abjured by patience
Waiting for recognition by forces highest
We overcome all obstacles to enrichment
For our universality un-assailed by negativity

Days of Days

mother oh mother lonely to face farther than a place
where many distances sew us together in pieces
stay in the holes in my heart and give me courage

to begin over from the shattered beauty of days

father oh father silent in your time of endurance
atop mountains of misery you keep the heart
beating by the burdens of keeping us free

to begin over from the silver sockets of days

god oh god invisible to our blindness
speaking through a haze of words
that we try so hard to sanctify

our love over and over from the pain of days

Love Inside Us

There's often the lapse between seed and flower.
Wisdom accrues with patience.
Or, patience accrues with age.

Sides of late summer roads abound with yellow hawk weed
standing tall between the blue chicory rubbing against
 wild sun flowers.
I often think of Oswego tea
 as a link to native peoples
using these flowers for healing beverages.

In the western part of America,
fire weeds lace roadsides
keeping me remembering beautiful landscapes.

We all are wildflowers
germinating our affection toward an invisible power
that created our magical patchwork of humanity.
My affection for beauty grows within me forever.
I cannot stop the odoriferous links to plants
that I have botanized or identified.
They are as permanent as my soul ever-lasting.
To separate these from my memory of love is impossible.

Patchouli covered skin slid off sex.
Marijuana infused itself into my sensory perceptions.
The isolated flowers of lovemaking are plants in my dreams.
Names fade but flowers of idyllic love never do.
There is no reduction of a fantasy becoming a reality with us.
Love is real against the windstorm of disappointment and regret.
Nothing is touched by divorce inside the gardens
of our love both visually and physically within us.

Sorrow

Come, tis but little time remaining
 for light to dim the shadows down
Come let loose that mantle of day
and slant thy eyes to heaven bound
We have taken fill of flowers
that lifted their petals slow with no sound
Let an earth swivel us to drowsy
and a moon finish us off to silence

I have refused the permanency
 of love in place of wonder
I have embraced the colors of your heart
I have been baptized by sorrow

Is there anybody out there

Is there anybody out there?
I am being shuttled through a life alone.
All my ex-wives have turned off my air supply.
None of my credit cards allow me any extra credit.
I seem to have the largest gas tank on earth when I fill up.
The charge for my medications would finance
rebuilding the Titanic.
My priest, rabbi and mullah have
rejected my sins as unforgivable.
My blood sugar levels are always close to putting me
into a diabetic shock.
My doctor wants me to explain to him why
I am so healthy but not yet dead.
If I go on a diet I gain weight.
If I eat less I gain weight.
If I eat healthy foods I gain weight.
Every time I change my will,
the people I have named or entrusted,
desert me including my attorney.

I have holes in all my socks.
I wear diapers that keep falling out of my pants
when I walk or shop.
I pray every night but never ever get an answer.
I have bad dreams with no good books to explain them.
I am an American of Arabic extraction
and I have added Buddhism to my Christian
and Muslim belief systems.
I have a John Deere seed cap,
a New York Yankees baseball cap
and a Jewish kippah or Yakama
in case Jesus comes back as a farmer,
a baseball player or a Jew.

Every one of my favorite poets, writers, philosophers,
painters and special people have all committed suicide.
I feel like a fish out of water, I feel like a boat without sails.

An engine without any gas. A car with no tires.
I pay too much tax. I earn too little money.

My budget stretches itself
over twenty continents and six planets.
Every check I write bounces off of fifteen
satellites and the rotating radar scope on the aircraft
carrier Enterprise.
When I finally get to sleep, I wake too early.
During the day I fall asleep in my chair
or while I am reading.

Clarity Of Prayer

The secret spell from music
that chants me into reverie.
Vespers of unintelligible languages
 that weave mysterious echoes.
Rachmaninoff creates, as well as Tchaikovsky,
choral magic out of sorrow.
Sounds of liquid nectar deepening us
to an inner peace of resignation.
My mother hears and holds me with rocking lullaby's.
My lover falls to silence hovering over me in requiems.
I am suspended in somber moons;
Held by faith in dark heavens;
Calmed by night's sacred stars;
Pulled away from heart-of-sadness;
Solved of life's enigmas by clarity of prayer
for fear of reprisals from idiomatic in sensitive's

Nocturne To Love

Evening clings to eyes
Fingers fold to emptiness
Across space dimmed stars salvage
what memories are left waiting for sleep
I am crossed in sanctity by passive breathing

It is all in nodding off to reverie
That calmness of forgetfulness
To put away the day in sachets
A perfumed drained to pillows
Where listing sails fold into night

My last thought is for ancient airs
Of slow streams wilting thinly as
Melodic serenades of Chopin

Close me into you as we meld
Like lovers who were famous

For Our Children

Caress softness
Words become real in defense
Imagery bathes the wounds of stench
We lay beside each other
Before a wall of death
Stops us from growing
Past our horror"

Blood ran out
Watering a tired soil.

The air received screams
impounding them to hell.

"My mother wherefore art thou?
Return us to the womb blessed."

Sam collected the dog-tags.
He clamped one inside teeth
and slung the other around his neck.
Sam never got over the terror in the eyes of the corpses.
He cautioned himself that he was giving final prayer
to his comrades.

"My mother I place myself in your hands
And hope this truly is the last war for our children."

Lips That Broke The Solemn Morn

They were called in whispers beaten
flickered shadows became so voiceless
lips that broke the solemn morn.

Sun-spattered dreams
in crimson eyes ...

Life was life.
Death is death.
Love and roses can answer them.

This place knows such woe
and tends to steep no mercy
as darkness-thick points its finger
the drench of sod in soiled earth
poor souls find no lasting hope
where kingdoms did once pretend.
The soldier's grave
the expense was spent
in lonely tomb
largeness comes in solemnitude
and my words went very silent:

Each warrior remains in his grave
I pray a rose fills his wilt today

Silted Sandy Bottomless Silence

We must have our ocean to see
what is in our hearts to be
in caverns of secret
dim lit sanctuary.

Quite as flagella
motioned by
currents of
swishes.

Waving brushed
to liquid
light.

Our neighbors are schooled
in gentleness and fury
of a landscape
buried in
layers.

Our eternity is above the waves
where a horizon beckons us.
But we stay safe below in
oceans of memories
of silted sandy
bottomless
silence.

By Death Shall I Conquer –
Per Mortem Vicero

By death shall I conquer
life's many pitfalls.
To hear but allay
pleasure's calls.

The hate, the love
as caution withdraws.
The push and shove,
all reason's flaws.

I am a wise fool
a silent clown;
Experience's tool;
A smile, a frown.

My thoughts outlast
my world's end.
Breaking at last
what desires portend.

See me smile
eyes open wide.
Sincerity's guile
is a loss of pride.

Watch me dissolve
as vapor or mist.
My life will evolve
by sweet tenderness.

Michael Thomas

In Some Frond Resting Place

We come apart into night's eye
swollen beside a virgin sense
of nobility of being.

We are fervent in hope.
Forgotten by littleness.

Our life squeezed -
platelets - condensed -
leaf scaled into sediment.

There never was a moon
glistening - on fire with imagination.
It was all so eventful and meaningless.

Do not be fooled by words
because they will fail us in the end.
It is only the sparsity of kindness
bolstering our fears as we slide.

Do not fret the poet's call.
It is like the loon crying by the water's edge
invisible by darkness
but there in essence in some frond resting place.

Rhyming Has Gone Astray

Humor can only come from minds in total disarray
Sadness is the place when joy has no place to stay
We wish that love not leave but eyes so often stray
Upon green fields lust's absent-mindedness is grey

Our histories remind us life is more than just today
The little worlds we live in confine us in every way
For happiness to remain we must always be gay
Then thoughts of clarity will rule us all the day

We have learned that love is like tooth decay
Plaque of affection builds and won't go away
We brush against each other like sore inlays
Divorces are dismal dramatic morality plays

Oh, it's just fine when we have first parity
Our coupling is an exhaustive fresh party
We fall asleep entwined in a half drowsy
Seen through windows we are propriety

But life draws a string - a necktie
We act out a scene of do-or-die
And each of us pretend to cry
In the end nowhere-or-why

Life is littleness - not big
Marriage is a tree twig
In gardens time digs
New loves from sprigs

Michael Thomas

Praying To The Gods Keeping My Bases Covered

Buddha, by Jesus, I love you to hell
Praying in chants like ringing a bell
I have my direction celled G P S
Turning my life over from a mess

Squared things with ex-spouse-y
Tax man left me empty trouse-y
Beard's gone. My ear ring too
Yarmulke pretending to be Jew

I wear sandals as Mohammad
Bowing to Mecca till I turn red
My heaven is a reincarnation
As a perfect act of contrition

Bless me Confucius for all sin
I confess humbly with a grin

The Rich

Elite constraint of pinnacle propriety
You know:
Spending their inheritance
Lonely in protected estates
But, always, living in abstention.

Didactic
Affrontive
Supercilious
Aloof
Arrogant
Argumentative in the way of absurdity.

Treasures of the rich include
maps of fishing sites long ago dried-up.

The horror of their commandments
are best thrown to pieces and go about
adoring any golden calves available.

You can imagine their expression of relief in organism
as donkeys braying or dinosaurs
with bronchial complications.

But being kind is always a forgiveness
for their conditions.

Always be quiet and never engage them
or you will lose sanity in-the-end.

Michael Thomas

A Requiem For The Non-Dead

When love ends there is a sadness
When hate ends there is a joy
Love creates a soul piece-by-piece
Hate obliterates a soul
When hate continues, there is no room for recovery
With love there is room for an eternity

All hate is a form of self-deprecation
The object of hate circles back to crush the hater
All the time spent hating is time wasted for loving

All the years spent with love were building years
When you left love in anger those years lost their value
What hate destroys takes as much time to rebuild from scratch

The soul is created bit-by-bit and expands by continued love
I have continuing love for you
Your absence is as if you are dead
So, I can love you through the veil
As if my love for you is a requiem
A requiem for the non-dead

First Voice: There is a sadness that escapes past reasoning
Second Voice: Say
First Voice: Like a montage of sorrow lilting as a banner
over a sullen sun set
Second Voice: Say
First Voice: I am taken by a voiceless wind into crevices of silence
Second Voice: Say
First Voice: On an echo of past extravagance
are less noise and more stretches of nothing

A Requiem For The Non-Dead Part 2

First Voice Alone: Can you be gay when the sky turns ash brown
and a lifeless forest crawls beneath an inescapable cloud

I am always alone by distances.
I turn and flowers fade to Fall's foliage.

Come into the room faint-lit
and sit among the place-mats of memories.

A requiem for the non-dead

Our Burnt Edges

Color me membrane morning mist
Take pigments from ancient skins
Relatives of bones left bleached
Into random swirls red-bled blue
Brought out clean by earth blown
Days reflected pottery brown ocher

Rest upon my hillocks of brush grass
Where deer left their dreams of stars

I am not dead but left to fly free
Atop a tree-line spent in solitude

Weave me embroidered by lace golds
Covering over a Friday feeling of lassitude

I am the tasks of Thursday pinned to a robin's breast
You will hear me whisper-wind tinkle of leaf and limb

Do not look for me but look for ice of constancy
We are frieze waiting of lots
We are the wonder of woven winters
Proving ourselves by patience under
The watchful eyes of so many gods
Who take pleasure in our deeds

We earn the respect of frogs
Atop a floating twig bark

There is green moss in our hearts
Left over happiness in our vapor trails
And tomorrow there will be rain
To take away our burnt edges of pain

Alone But Never Lonely

I could be the color of overripe avocados
Adhering to scandals of dark semblances.

I disappear in shadows.

All my lovers reached for me with eyes closed
A camaraderie of soul mates
Flinching at danger
Never deserting.

In moonlight spilled upon
cool Nile banks, I overflowed.

Pyramids rose into place
centuries collected as stones -
My heart hardened
From indifference.

While caravans slept
I enjoined the stars
Silent to a fault.

Have you ever wished for death?
Been rewarded by a full life?

Tomorrow I will return my borrowed eyes.
To scales of justice I concur a balance.

To those who see me, let them lower their voices
And turn aside out of courtesy
To a prejudice of ignorance.

I am alone but never lonely.

Michael Thomas

Ancient Memories

This loveliness of words pauses my breath
stalls all who read with wonder eyes.

We leave broken icicles of thoughts
in a stream linked by our senses.

Come to the corridors of light
opening hearts to hope.

We are temporary / magnificent
Once beautiful forever timed.

The bones of our celebrations
keep faith in a wind of mercy.

Hear ancestors welcoming us
with tears and bounty joy.

There is never a wrinkle
within ancient memories.

Footprints

I told wind - cover all you can
turbulent reminder of terror

Let there be waves ocean-less
of leaf, limb stormy rage

Remind us of peace
awaiting finality

Whisper to me such of uncovered madness's.

I will make ready places where silence rules
cathedral-like below arched entrances

There the little ones scamper playfully
Here footprints line black river beds
thick in soppy clay evidence

I told wind - tell me of origins
cold avenues thawing into spring canopies
Let me into secret aromatic lilac wishes

Find You Forever

ancients wait for us to come out and teach us
like stories of the fish we never caught
or the mountains we never climbed
they keep us mesmerized by their words

the old rise up from their graves and try to shock us
by their elemental scary visages and grimaces
as they warn of danger or consequences of our acts

sitting on papa's ashes I feel the weight of his world
the dead lie upon us like dirt over our coffin
while we are still alive, they try to smother us

everywhere I look the beauty overwhelms me
the sound of wind and rain soothes me
the wish of trees blowing like wild horses
makes me feel all the distances of time

the old cannot rise up because they are only bones
the past is a remembrance of empty imaginations
it is now that I feel the ice of winter or breath of spring
the torrents of time tick me to sleep by crickets singing

I am my brother of generations who wished to be me
I am the last summer of their broken dreams
I am me atop the pile of evolution sandwiched below me
I am the sweet end of days and nights of dying sunsets
Cover me over with a thin veil of mist so I can awake
and feel the little joys of fingers and legs moving aimlessly
I am the spirit of love collecting over you with passion
bringing you to understand how much I find you forever

Papa and the Moon

papa don't crack his bones
hair like white chicken's
bleached eyes sad blue

mama she cares less
than those days gone

papa he laid his gun
against the barn wall
watched for night fall
crossed in shadows

can't tell the difference
tween grey cow patty
from closed back door

papa he turned old
like chipped paint
dusty leaf mold
won't buy more stars
or the sky empties
of all it's memories

papa will seal up his time
in his eyes no light arrives.

Michael Thomas

Unending Measure

I do not know how or why I loved God,
but from my age of reason at five or six,
I begin to see the power of creation in all things around me.
My family were indifferent to my fervor.

My friends never understood the clarity with which I feel
and know the great spirit force that surrounds
us with love and protection.
As a six year old,
I simplified my understanding
by thinking that all people knew God as I felt God.
I prayed every day to the veil that kept God hid from our eyes.

The purity of love through the curtain of time
always ends up with God on the invisible levels
above and below and around us.
The God who keeps us from colliding with disaster is my God.
My God creates havoc to some people but,
for some reason, not for me.

As a growing human being,
I learned to keep secrets of shadows to myself.
I learned to keep the mysteries of sound,
silence and mistiness quietly inside my soul.
 I learned that I do have a soul.
My soul is the piecemeal composite
of all the good things I do for myself and for others.
My soul is the growing nodule of sanctity
put together like a puzzle inside my heart.
My soul vibrates with all the acts of kindness
that make up my days of light.

I can only tell you that my soul is made up
of all the things I have given up or given to others in my life.
I have a soul of gifts.
I only give to others that which I love enough
to place in other peoples' possession.

If I give a gift, it is something I love so much
and I will only give that gift to others to vibrate
in their lives with the love I felt for the gift.

There is no secret to my childhood turning into adulthood.
It happens so swiftly and holds itself into place for eternity.
My adulthood is my clarity of soulfulness that abides
side-by-side with my invisible God that I trust in and love
with unending measure.

Red Inside Our Tenuous Lives

Of course, if you are a street person
living in the imaginary world
of fetid waft rising up,
threatening to choke ice cream marble pigeons
who cough beneath the acrid veil
of shadowed crowded streets, then, and only then,
your blood is rinsed by harbor water stench
and is grey by indifference to breathing to survive.

Somewhere in the line of evolution,
you fit into chaos of civilization whose lack of sewers
led to vomit green drippings hanging from rat filled drains.
Then your blood was still grey, exactly like today.
I remember begging the whore
who walked away from my entreatments
to picnic with me in the country.

I pleaded with her to escape
before death covered over her nakedness
of crushed bread crumb skin.
She had the blood of a prisoner
of her own war and coughed like the pigeons
in phlegm as she threw her fag into the steaming iron metal grill
where the street became invisible
to the gush of rain washed blood.

Oh, we have all lay beneath the trunk risen tree
of chestnut shimmer
and felt the clean wind of a park hidden from the city.
Here is where our blood was the color of cheap wine
staining our lips asleep inside our hearts.
But do not be misled.
Those times were crowded into the history of evolution
circling itself like a snake
around the birth and death of caution.
We knew that there was no other color to blood
but red inside our tenuous lives.

Jesus And The Blues

Jesus was a lover of the eastern sky when it shook loose the stars.
Across the Mediterranean he wished for whales swimming in salt.
He swore to himself to bring bread to the poor and milk to babies.
His mother hoped he would find some peace before he got too old.
Jesus watched the fishermen come to relax and take whores.
He knew the hearts of heaven would pardon their indiscretions
So, he turned his eyes away from the laughter, letting day end.

Jesus carried truth in small parts of his memory to ease his pain.
He never let the swell of ignorance turn him away from compassion.

Jesus was at home with love. He felt his best when he pardoned.
It was hard for Jesus because the majority of people,
all of which he loved, were so preoccupied with life
that very few could see the larger picture of God and
all the faith that was lost from their distractions.

We let the lies take us into dark places and we cry when we lose.
We know that the night will not cover over our driving desires.
We grow weary asking for forgiveness so we learn to smile.
When the collision of earth-to-heaven brings us some sense
Then there is blue in our hearts and blue in our eyes of love.

Jesus painted the eyes of the world blue and went to sleep
with blues in his dreams to keep us feeling good about life.

What Was Here

We hear what was gone but came back with melody
of Bach's "Matthew" that comforts us in Christianity.

Later on we are visited by Buddha who approves
of the adulation of his brother who took the pressure
off, and let the world see language of salvation.

There was no reason for you to believe in the crucifixion
since there were so many zealots who professed messiah.

Ad agencies of now speak of what was here for us to believe.
We close our eyes and are led down a golden path of promises.

Jesus came back from India when the news spoke
of him who was here.
He met with his friends and broke bread for their bodies
and gave them words for their souls:
"Remember I am with you for all time.
Close your eyes and speak my name
for I will appear and comfort you with my lasting love."
The apostles tried passing this down and failed out of dilution
of belief. That is: We believe until something else sounds better
and allows us to forget the past of "What was there"
compared to "What was here" for us to grasp forever.

The Forests of Yesterday

Lonely like sunsets laying across forgotten horizons
Bird singing ended and trees sitting waiting for night
The singular owl being alone for pair calling hoping
Into the hollow tree stump of squirrel havens
Out of the bush of raccoon hunger emerges

These inconsequential creatures spilling out
of nature's scenery not caring for maps or guides.

She left me like a bird who knows where to fly
not caring whether I was sad or glad for her to go.

Between life and love she went quickly away
and the golden grey morning cried with me.

Could I be a beaver and care nothing for dams.
Could I be a hawk and not know how to hunt.

I was a lover who fell out of the net of love
A special person who lost all my specialty.

Keep me from the cold of indifference.
Let me peer out of the hollow tree trunks.
My borders have all been crossed and
My lessons have been turned over in my mind.

Could I have been kinder? Wiser? A little smarter?
All I have left behind are in the forests of yesterday.

Michael Thomas

Everything New

come sing me a sparrow's sadness tree limb hovel of anguish
let loose the drama rattling around the hollows of your heart
tenderness settles itself over vibrations of tears and mistrust
allow chorus's cover to last long into echoes of ministrations

we wait limbo's shadowed entrances spilling themselves blue
ointments of vicarious messages fill up the caverns of night

I remember your innocent ribbon banners flagged in light
you have lost no glamour as excitement surrounds pieces of you

worthiness puffs into all you give to the world of grace and love

heart's left over delicacies sandwiched between sorrows
lay down beside spent passion of eyes closed in trust
we will outlast the days and begin again forgotten

Through A Silent Moment He Whispered To Me

Through A Silent Moment He Whispered To Me,
through slanted windblown silent waving trees.
I closed my eyes to look inward so I could see
lasting remnants of a day letting-up in degrees.

A piano played Rachmaninoff second movement
of concerto number two in C-Minor, Opus eighteen.
It was a direct line to my god that I felt and heard
music beyond music that opened up my soul.

Nothing remained in residue of anxiety or hurt
as each turn of the music swept me away.
Never before had I floated above myself
expanding in an umbrella of light and love.

We are told that being born is much harder
than dying when we follow the fibers holding us.
The wishing for completion is fulfilled
in the deliverance of our hearts out of our body.

Time dissolves. We let go of ourselves into arms
of safety. The succor of our creator heals us.
We are like a module re-fixing ourselves to a core.
We are made to the image and become re-attached.

The highest forces of clarity instill us with gratitude
and we join ancestors of ages, our god-of-all-gods
placing us within the echoes of a faceless whisper.

Michael Thomas

Starting All Over

Our grandfathers are farther away
Than our ancestors here today
They hear our yearnings
And all we think or say

We are linked back to the ape,
Small or large creatures who gape
Into the star splintered sky of night
That we wonder at with such delight

The world around us is wrought
With hope we paid for or fought
Till our bloodless bones condensed
Into soiled ice cave's mysteries end
Poetry is just another nature's joke
Ridding us of comedy that we poke
At the sliding wake of humanity
Here or just going up in smoke

Many religions hold us in sway
As we kneel, bow our heads to pray
But we do not give up till we die
Then start over all the things we try

It's Only a Miracle

daddy is dead and mamma is waiting her turn
there is moisture coming from their eyes
like tears wetting the linen of dead mummies

I noticed the emptiness without them guiding me
I am here in the dark and watching their mystery dissolve

there is very little left but emptiness of light

we all go to the same place upon dying,
the sacred rooms of sleepiness

I would rather be alone
as the world keeps it's pace

seems like our insecurities get set aside
and we carry our privacy into the grave

there is a whole lot more to welcome us across the veil
it's only a miracle
and we take it for granted
as the crying of the souls
covers over our fears

it's only a miracle
and we collect stars
before the morning
comes to welcome us

Michael Thomas

War

At the start it was fun as a young man's fantasy of adventure. Like high school sports recognition for the exceptional - war was the giving back for family members who returned from Europe World War II, with a sense of pride.

The delving into the unknown of volunteering for Vietnam without any concept of Asian peoples' culture or history. The French being driven out of South East Asia was a "non-sequitur" to the ignorance of us soldiers.

In the orientation room, upon landing in Vietnam, incoming soldiers were given prophylactics and told to keep from having children. No mention was made of fighting conditions or terrain. It amazed me that sex was more important than fighting.

We flew into the isolated army base by helicopter. Our assignments were handed out and each of us established ourselves in the barracks quarters.

Vietnam is an oasis of Asian loveliness with rich green rubber plantations, distant horizons of rice paddy beauty spread like a water-spill into the low areas of the greenish fresh land. Water buffalo stood up to their bellies submerged. Half naked people bent over pulling rice out of the mirrored shimmering puddled surfaces. Figures with sun shield round straw hats looked up as we walked past. We would learn, later, how these people lived without any of the conveniences we are used to.

Each living hut was occupied by men sorted out by their occupation. All the belly gunners who rode astride the helicopter open doors with their guns on mounts, lived in one barracks. The ground troops, who went out on patrol each day, lived in another barracks. The army called these small barracks "hooches". The army had a name for everything.

remember how social contact was held in meetings in one particular hooch when men got together and oiled and cleaned their guns. The banter and exchange of firearms took place while they drank and smoked. Everybody on the compound seemed to relish having

side arms strapped on their waist as they walked around all day. It was as if they were cowboys and guns were their self-security. In another particular hooch it was a regular weekly slide show or movie of all the people that had been killed during the week. Men would relish looking at images of dead boys and soldiers tied up and heads hanging down or shot off. It was the most gruesome unholy thing I ever encountered. It was total barbarism.

There are so many stories in my memory of nights of flares, red tracer bullets leaving a trail of lines where bullets found their targets. I spent one whole year with this fighting and nothing in my life compared to finally flying home to try to forget the noise and mayhem and dead bodies.

Your Smile a Salvation

Immobile in somber death forgot
You lay as warriors bloated bier
Eyes closed, scant breathing
Imploded in secret dreams

My fear is you are forsaken
By derelict gods out of fashion
Intransigent angels black burnt
By cold fires of hell's constraint

A mockery of your savage tongue
In days past your vitriol scathing
Against featherless vagabonds
Deserving not your benedictions

All gone beside dried ocean streams
Of fish boned deserts skin shriveled
To whorled sand storms desiccation
Adventure-less you sleep infamous

My tears collect by indifference
My prayers die at their roots
I wipe your forehead sweat brow
And give you my best last rites

The tree has severed roots
The earth replaces itself
My memory keeps laughing
With your smile a salvation

In silence and tears,
Half broken-hearted
To sever for years,
Pale grew thy cheek and cold,
Colder thy kiss;
Truly that hour foretold
Sorrow to this.

The dew of the morning
Sunk chill on my brow--
It felt like the warning
Of what I feel now.
Thy vows are all broken,
And light is thy fame;
I hear thy name spoken,
And share in its shame.

They name thee before me,
A knell to mine ear;
A shudder comes o'er me--
Why wert thou so dear?
They know not I knew thee,
Who knew thee so well--
Long, long I shall rue thee,
Too deeply to tell.

In secret we met--
In silence I grieve,
That thy heart could forget,
Thy spirit deceive
If I should meet thee
After long years,
How should I greet thee?--
With silence and tears.

Michael Thomas

Being so Mean

sometimes empty
sometimes clean
longing for someone
not so mean

days without sun
nights with no one
longing for a queen
not so mean

remember tomorrow
was same as today
we grew up different
not so mean

time is a mountain
piled high in dreams
see everything below
keeping us above
being so mean

sadness is blessing
making us wiser
charity is our lesson
helping us rise above
being so mean

often I am alone
never lonely
you are my prayer
my earthly angel
never mean

Vastness

There have been times when things stopped around me, like, totally stopped. I paused to sense what was happening and briefly closed my eyes. Deep in the recesses of some part of me that remains hidden, most all the time, a reverberation of stillness hums as an electrical disconnect.

It is uncanny, to say the least. It is an opening to a layer of reality as in an unexplored vacuum that can be frozen then come back to life thawed bit-by-bit in a dynamic balance of wordless containment.

This "State Of Awareness" is depth-less in shadows of silver oracles. I can become part of this entrapment as long as I do not try to control it. I must let the pillow of content hold me within its mystery. I must give up all thought and allow the ambiance of this query become a part of me immersed within this wolf stare of becoming.

I have experienced this phenomenon in instantaneous crisis when I was held between worlds in emergencies such as car accidents or within the bellows of warfare during exploding shells and death surrounding me in an exhale of bombastic silences.
A force of gentleness emerges during these hiatuses. A force so spiritual engulfs my heart with precious love so healing in its confluence.

It is a love not part of time or motion. It is a love of feeling free to want all that can be given in a way that I want only to give back what is given to me.

In this state of profundity I glaciate into bluish clarity. I become, as if, emptied of myself and inhabiting an unknown persona. It is beyond elevation or geometric spaciousness. I feel like a sojourner or pilgrim of a vastness breathless in its scope.

Awakening to Hope

It is far too early to judge humanity
Collectively dissolved in blood
True-or-false in intentions
Indiscernible by immersion
Into a wish-wash of sunsets.

By weight of charity versus hate
Various histories lie still as stone
And no epithet suitable devised.

It is a compilation of feather-fall
Sandwiched between glaciers.

Certainly confounded
Blindly in a balance
Of confidence in justice.

The swing factor toward ablution
Is a faint breath of Eve expiring
By degrees favorable in poetics.

Hear a whisper of silence
Winning over as planets subside.

It is always only kindness that
Awakens our hearts to hope.

Our Gentle Hearts Throb With Praying

Tis not the dead that speak of living
It's us that need the act of forgiving

Life returns in circles of unknowing
All futures depend on who is giving

Bestir thyself with hope in deriving
The memory of our souls arriving

Oh! Sweat of humanities striving
For equanimity's newest devising

Lay hate to rest, pick up appraising
Our gentle hearts throb with praying

Less words, more silence in saying
That peace within us never delaying

The object in life is to live weighing
What death means for us surviving

Blood Test

She loves me, she loves herself, keep it to yourself.
Love is fickle and she is as capricious as an elf.
Tomorrow will find her eating at another plate,
Today we find her posing for a picture on a date.

Ah! The apple does not fall far from the tree.
Men picking up her dress, see what they see.
A whole lot of trouble comes from innocence,
Forsaking wisdom on our knees in penance.

But, big the game, so small the just rewards,
Enter jungle wild as lions, leave as cowards.
We men will boast holding up joyous cheer,
But, her parents will pull us off by our hair.

The family conspires to have us gone.
The doctor joins us, our genes belong.

In Fondling Youth Allays Time to Spare

In fondling youth allays time to spare
Nor flower fades nor aspiration flies
Into the link where continuity lies
Innocent where angels do not care

Slowly how the mind sweetly knows
Little clues awareness builds a nest
Excluding less, including but the best
In gardens weedless love but grows

Time erodes confidence season's lust
Turns cold winter minds to sleep anon
Buried beneath leaf-of-life all begone
In heaven's heart plied doubt-to-dust

There were burdens broken and bent
But sealed within our soul's testament

The Rabbi Prays

For the night wind spaced between heaven's scent,
Wherever you are Adonai I am with you in spirit.

Out of the stretched silences of the dark desert sands
silted through their shifting elements, I bless you,

Here in the vacancy of my heart I wait for your presence
to fill me with healing ointments of empathy and wisdom.

My Adonai who sends all emissaries of angels to tend to me.
My Adonai who collects me into patient corners of ease.

Baruch atah Adonai elohaynu melech ha'olam asher
kidshanu bemitzvotav vetzivanu l'hadlik ner shel Shabbat.

When the stars bring light to my eyes, it is you I see Adonai
When the spilling of emptiness covers the heavens, it is you.

Out of the fear of my insecurities I seek your guidance.
In my humble way of restraint I trust in your protection.

My Lord of differences who subjects me to the particular
I select the finest words that will please your ears and
speak them on paper to you with music of the wistful sounds.

My Lady god of mixtures who is my Adonai angel,
I swear to allegiance of your mysteries.
My Adonai of woman magics', please grant
me the grace of your thoughts forever.

I am never sure of my homages.
I am always in debt to your gifts.
I begin and continue with your aid.
My Adonai of angels who dusts my eyes with desert soil
I pray in simple presence of your elixir of aperitif.

You are the after echo of snow fall
across the glacial connections
entwined between mountains
in blue specter ice.

I am the whisper of syntactical psalms.
Hear me Oh lady of mercies.
Bless me with gold amber
shadows of evenings dew.

Displacement

When I am in a crowd I remember my hatred of being crowded
into association of closeness with people who are uncomfortable
with solitude of emptiness where all conversation is unnecessary.
 Overly touchy souls who seek not to know underlying realities
portraying false self-confidence as if their presence is sufficient
to overcome the intimacy of the savage poet's observances.
 Having my sun sign in the twelfth house of the Babylonian system,
I prefer being alone as the most efficient way to serve others. My
preference for quiet extends itself out to expanses of
lonely deserts or that restful space between star groups.

I learned to enjoy cafeterias where the noise of discussions
allowed me to not single out any one voice but the unhindered
avenues of nothingness so easy to lose myself within in thought.
If you were to compare me to the wary beast cautious for danger
or the tiny rodent who can single out any impending enemy,
then selecting the one animal for me would have to include
all creatures who protect themselves by exclusion.

Therefore I am a consciousness of specialty
with a soul of distinctness as if self-contained
within an ego that displaces definitions
for extreme self-preservation of forever.
I try hard at patience toward ignorance.
Being kind to the unwary fool
Is my most delicate balance
since I am more than often
them by displacement.

Two Minute Warning - Fourth And Goal

Time collects in back slaps of camera dizzy seconds.
Little did we know the immediacy of ex-spouses or enemies
of valor-less sympathies.
The neighbor we avoided lines up against us.

Weather is bad. History is silent in the doorway to death.
There are no previews or special last minute heroics.

Erase the childhood hope for redemption.
Our mother is not here to defend us.

I remember how climbing had temporary resting camps
as the wind tore the flaps of our tents open
like some invisible god was angry at our achievements.

Each morning we moved up with renewed hope.
But now there is no precipice above us.
Thunderbolts split the air.
Rain and snow pelt us.

We exchange glances;
Shut out all meaningless prayer.
It is only ourselves that we face as the veil splits open
leaving ragged ends of scrolls with their ink dripping
into the crevices of our eyes waiting for a desert to dry.

Michael Thomas

Fire Of My Soul

"Sky above me - Earth below me - Fire within me" -
A Viking Saying

Somewhere between a star and air I breathe
I leave a slipstream for you to follow me.
Limits of my arms becoming wings constrain me.
You are my star reaching to rise me above the world.

I sink below the permafrost in hibernation.
My soul is tired and rests in silence with you guarding me.

Here in the emptiness of sleep there is eternal life within me

as a kindle of hope that aspires to be born over-and-over.
Like the earth, I have a core fire remaining from my creation.
It is the magnet of what binds me to you in similarity.
It is my soul lit forever in unison with an invisible force.

File Me Away

All poets rise above the soup of ordinary.
Scan library's shelves of wonderment
and we are insignificant in scale like
constant freeway traffic or that slow
up-down of persistent suns taking
their cue from their solar gods.
All poets trust in their recognition
by invisible forces that brought
them into existence and will
waste them away to death's inexorable time degradation.
All poets intuit the folly of ego and mock the shallow kind.

The words of poets in their finery
dressed like prim-and-proper
adornment, taking imagery
to the highest level of their
imaginations - these words
are vain attempts to describe
what can only be felt - these
words that add to creation's
further elaboration of reality.
I am face-down humble to
even be called a poet.
I always wait for the shoe to fall upon me,
or the voice out of the clouds denouncing
me as a fake , making me tremble in shame.

Even as I write at the best, I am the worst.
You, my poet friend, are my judge.
I sing to you like a bird of unconscious.
I bail you out of obscurity by my presence.
I furnish you with a benchmark of status.
Label me, staple me, file me away in your memory.

Michael Thomas

Waiting

Well, I am waiting around this heaven
Waiting for some magic to place
Within the bosom of everlasting.
 I am tired of trying to chase the devil
Out of my heart of wariness.
I am waiting for a message
Like Ezekiel in the desert
Seeing faces in the sand.
 I am madly electric.
Suspended chant.
Train conductor-less.
Shiftless ship-less captain-less.

My hope is diminished by all the pain
of worldly craziness.
Even in my solace I worry about the
 danger of radicalization.
So, I pray -
Jesus you are my rock and roll.
Jesus you are my conductor.
Jesus you are my engineer.
Buddha you bring me to quietness.
Confucius you teach me to love my neighbor.
I am waiting around the bus station.
I am waiting around the airport.
I have a ticket to salvation
and I am bringing you along with me.
Yea! The two of us will
pass through the veil of innocence
and enter the portals of Valhalla
where all the gods will welcome us.

River Eyes

skies grey down drizzle asphalt rivers bend
my eyes blur tunnels spiraling never to end
surely our homes are dissolved by all dread
but hear sparrow's sorrow song's joy instead
colors burnt coils within leafless trees spent
rivers tear themselves till death must repent

Beatitude Of Mercy

It takes a lot of trouble to be a poet.
One has to spin the world a ball-bearing.
Smote the wind with northern whimsy.
Single out hawk's cry from trees sowing.
Bring out heaviness, cure it, reinvent.

I lack luster to shimmer oceans.
Have not strength of rooted oaks.
Pale beside Autumn's technicalities.

There was a chemist extraordinary.
His potion killed the one he loved.
But, she became perfect for the grave.
He became perfect for regret.
That's poetry, like Patroclus's envy.

I carry the burden of history
in dungeons of despair.

I live again for Christian ontology.

Impressions of heroes wax thin.
I never tell those I admire
for fear they will dissolve.

My cave of isolation
immures me captive.

Love pours forth from my chakras.
Recipients never are asked returns.
Why would one ask the moon mercy?

We Were

follow the forest edge
where we slept nights away
there was honor to our feelings
an honesty of touches
then the trees came to an end
an ocean swallowed us whole
and spat us out into emptiness
in the morning we were forgotten

Precious Memories

precious memories
lay in lacquer
on scales
of time
keep
me

beautiful listen
to unseen birds
hidden in song
from our eyes

when all is lost
all is found
in favor
of our
eyes

travel two roads
leave ourselves
between worlds
spiral into edges
of fruit so sweet

no god can deny
how hard we try
to be better off
than before we
started singing
mandolin sparks
joy within us

precious sacred
little space of love
splintered to gold
embers of echoes

we are given rest
among the boughs
of silver branches
with those birds
father's feathers
hide us safely
in precious

You, Three Times Love

night in your eyes asleep
crickets awake to my ears
tomorrow waiting restless

summer alive by frog call
serenading a full house moon
to a heart emptying a loneliness

Autumn blooming
fanfares of flowers afire
color of your eyes of desire

My Success Becomes My Failure

When a person sells themselves to another person
or gives themselves over totally to an idea or belief
then they become "self-less" in the true sense.
They no longer have a "self-image" to cling to.
They no longer are a person in control of themselves.
They become a puppet to their ideology.
They forgo their right to their own soul.
They cannot write honestly,
speak honestly or act as an individual.
All their actions revolve around pleasing their indenture.
They are fixed like an addict to the object of their slavery.
They know it. They are so obvious yet oblivious.
The heart of an empty person is a black vessel.
Their heart is no longer filled with charitable deeds.
I do not judge. I only report what I see as a poet.
I will not be part of any group or accept points from anyone.
I hold my own contests from my own points.
I judge my contests as impartially as possible.
Do not get me wrong - I am still an asshole idiot.
I try so hard to rise above my inanity
And, if I say I succeed, then I have failed.

10-Deadliest-Wars-in-Human-History

It is beyond our imagination that history is within our perspective.
History unfolds the magnitude of horror of war and its effect.
We cannot comprehend the scope of suffering to peoples.
We read and try to understand what forces unleash death.
If murder is so rampant in history, how do we count resurgence?
There can only be one avenue of human population - reincarnation.
Our humankind deaths pale in comparison to our human populations.

There is no justification for war's injustice to civilian populations.
The intensity of population growth is a force against human suffering.

There are now more people on the earth than ever has been in history.
We have reached an demarcation point of not having enough food.

As a writer and poet, I can only draw one conclusion to history:
We cleanse ourselves by attrition in wars and natural disasters.
And, in the process, historically, there is no distinction between
 civilians and soldiers. We are one in growth and one in death.

Light That Has Survived

Throw thyself - cold ice will not free sacrifice
nor follow your intentions to hellish paradise.
You are but a grief-ridden sod of sodomite,
A layer of leaf bleached-brief vacant erudite.

Suns of sorrow, bitter tastes of moon's wake
How little we grow with less than we can take.
But fear not, thy velvet cloak of invisibility
will strip away pretension taking any purity.

How salvation depends upon lasting mercies
when fear silences disgust in small travesties.
There is the road left open by wishing the best
and march, we do, toward all we do so detest.

We are leaving an earth better than we arrived:
Breathless gestures of light that have survived.

The Cat Without A Christmas

I will tell you a cat of Christian
faith known a cusp of Christmas
found scrapping near dumpsters
singing choral "inspiritus" cheers.

Never to tell its faithless roots
Abandoned by saints and crooks.

Stare, you might, out-stare its eye
Never blink though blink you try
For it is in the zone beyond us
Where devotees don't discuss.

Soul, it has with no fixation
To church or school tradition.

This cat with no name or religion
Sometimes snatches a loose pigeon.

No mercy is ever extended
Nor good will ever intended.

We can give it a smile so true
As it is only a cat who knew
How to handle living alone
Without a hearth or home.

I Wanna Be With You

Wanna find you in the fingers of strings of suns
reflecting off of rivers flowing into the night.

Follow you down the streams of silence
as they travel from the slips of dripping
waterfalls of golden sparkles like eyes
of smooth airless droplets of water.

Take me through the forest and let me loose in lakes and oceans.
Take me through the plains of dryness and creature's footprints.
Bless me with your graces like little dreams of moist pools.

Find me with you in dew morning mentioned lips of hunger.
There is blood in my eyes. There is salt in my tears.
There are halos saintly around my heart of yearning for you.
I call to the wolf of mystery. I wait for the hidden eyes
half mad in the misty lagoons of leaves and shadows.

I come up for air with my sins let go into the river Jordan.
I let go of all my hopes with one touch of your fingers.
I wanna go to whoever is left to feel or remaining after
all others have disappeared into the layers of rocks.

Come with me to the little lakes of loneliness
and we will dip into the chemistry of salvation.

Michael Thomas

Heaven

Maybe there is a heaven. If there is, I can only imagine the reward for people. I call it a reward, but it could well be a punishment. We tend to refrain from bad language when someone does us a discourtesy. We are so careful to be sure that we are not criticizing something we are guilty of. It would be hard to see myself rushing to get ahead of others in line. The faces of brutish people ignore looking at surrounding grimaces as they hurry up and push ahead as if they were on a critical mission. We do silently say to ourselves: "Bastard".

But we never speak it aloud. I have a secret wish for a laser pistol that makes people disappear, if they offend me. But, I know that all my relatives and social group on the other side of the veil would hate it if I sent jerks to them. Out of courtesy, I would laser a few nice people so as to please my ancestors. It isn't as if my relatives are perfect. I would laser Uncle Joe on the other side and send him back to earth. Joe was a very weak man with a face of a dissolute savage. He had a terribly twisted nose and ear from the gangsters beating him up for not paying his bets.

My uncle had a rancid smell. It was a deep fragrance of mold like where worms live. I could well imagine him on a hook as bait for whales. We would have to attach his brother Tony on multiple splitter lines for trawling. The two brothers were reprehensible. They were thieves. They spoke out of turn and never spoke of anything important. They both would remind people of what little favor they gave as a continual hope for hand-outs.

Ancient Lore

I come across time ticking
Molecules humming against the stillness
A beehive of invisible whispering

Less the world forget itself in sleepiness
Awake in loneliness
Like the blink of a bat upside-down
Or the "pair-calling" of the owl, echoing across centuries

I recall ponds alive with frogs and peepers suspended
above loon's choral, silver night shadows
The distance from branch to water as the kingfisher dives

Oh! And the surprised croak of the grouse
coming out of the wet weeds of bulrush
flailing themselves to a secret wind

There were the chirp of dozing tree birds
dreaming safely behind leaf cover
and the famous sweep of hawk wing plunging
with hunger driven talons

I love this world within worlds –
page-by-page volumes of ancient lore

New Year's Poem

Calm pervades
Eyes screen gray semblances
Fingers loosen thinned threads of emptiness

It was only yesterday that I loved you
I am resigned to your disappearance
In little cubes of thoughts,
 you sifted between the rocks gathered in stillness

Here is where your breath left a vapor on my neck
Here a sense of your body wilted to garlands of aching
Why did the excitement of you become so lonely

I will change the dates of forgetting
Before angels entangle themselves in sleep
I will become a spirit of forgiveness,
 taking away what pain is left over
and wish you a new year built upon
so many yesterdays of love

A Chant Poem

my presence is perchance neither here nor there in time
for I am howabalita no mo freestray la la la la la la la la
moshasha sho drapoala
du pre da pray made
muntro mundi my heart lets you into its chambers

so ho padatra mdua matro
mun u shor ma mati
shianti mungula pardeeeeeee
shama shuma ma ha putre

ungggggggggggggggggggg
matra
deeee
propa noti
mata junga do lasee
procee u we shwee

let the slow sound of chant
take me to stray lands of mystery

puptu matri
undo la la la la la la la la la la

soda sostria padu prayu
sogot pro naryee no most per day

I am lost in the purdu paya
I am shut out by shuti nyra nu

sad among the mongo shiva sat suranday

Michael Thomas

I wonder

So many nights
before morning comes
Laying breathless
in sleepless agitation
I hear a voice and it is not yours
or any person I know, so I pray:
Take away my sight since I am alone
and do not need to see
Give me a weight to lay heavy
on my soul since I am a sinner
So many nights
before the day begins
I wonder where is peace in my heart
and do I have to die to finally rest in your arms.
Take away my hearing because I need silence to cover me over.

Take away the time because
it is worthless to me to feel the minutes
or feel the uselessness of words of comfort.
Take away the hours.

I wonder if you have doubts and do you cry for comfort.

I am not blessed nor do I mourn for comfort
I wonder why do you allow me to feel pain
that I did not cause or wish for.
So, I wonder and I wish
for a different lesson to come to me

I wonder where is my friend - sleep
Where is that angel that dusts my eyes drowsy
Where is that force of peace that gives me comfort.

I wonder Aloud

Blessed are they who mourn,
for they shall be comforted.

... When?

Life

I write because I have to
There's no other way out
Life presents itself to do
What's right and never pout
What's wrong is to be unkind
When others break the rules
You try to pay them no mind
For ignorance has no clues

A fool can be an asshole
Speaks in forked tongue
Their egos are a grass full
Of snakes hid among-
Among a desert rain
Collected into pools
Along barren terrain
Dust spiraled spools

Elastic night besides
Silted Silver moons
Lizards shed hides
Wind whisper dunes
I forgive, try to forget
My pain won't erase
Devils from my heart
Dark from my face

Life is never black or white
Experience teaches us to wish
For peace and never to fight
For to love is to live in bliss

Being Reborn

When I awake to a new morning, I feel reborn.
It takes a bit of time for my eyes to clear
  as well as my mind getting focused.
I know that re-birthing happens
  in several manners:
Letting a preacher dip your head as a congregation sings
Letting a doctor tell you your test results
I felt so reborn after my divorce.
I had thought of changing my name out of celebration.
I get the feeling of being new when I pay off a credit card in full.
If my gas gauge reads empty and I make it home safe,
I breath a relief.
One of the most important times to be reborn
is after a great meal with a small glass of wine.
I will tell you the most vivid time I was born again
was when the mortar rounds stopped falling and,
amid all the dead bodies, I was still alive.

Forsaken

Damned innocence cloaking love blind
Spread thin over unwary hearts of trust.
Dissuading desire from cautions kind
Encouraging dark reality burning lust.

Oh! The touch of skin, kiss of fire
Couples moaning, eyes closed to light.
Sweet taste of sweat, passion desire
Clouding over sense of wrong-from-right.

Thus asleep dust whispering angels tell
Wind to waken curtain windows wide.
Sleepless walls to close out nights spell
And show tableau of what lovers hide.

How we oft turn and run from truth
Forsaking deeds a devil does forsooth.

The Peacemakers

Crying wounded in a wilderness of solitude.
Tears for history confounded by mayhem.
Torn life from all pages of decency as the
cat left in the rubble of orphans alone.
I have seen bullets come out the other side of surprise.
Shrapnel leaving holes in the hearts of innocence where
light of an errant god shines aimlessly into night.
No longer do we trust Robert Schumann's fantasie:
"Langsam Getragen: Durchweg Leise Zu Halten"
Please forgive me from romanticism such as
blessed are the wishes of the peacemakers
for they shall be nailed to the wall of destiny.
We all will go to our death in deprivation.
There will be no "Flights of angels sing thee to thy rest!
And why does the drum come hither?" - For sweet repose
to blot out the memory of Priam or the pain of Achilles.
Take the tablets from Sinai. Turn them into dead sea scrolls
that cannot be read for fear of reprisals. The lord speaks
through the mouths of wayward elders who have no faith.
Like children whose voice is lost amidst the tracer fire,
we are the peacemakers who walk blind into napalm.

Comfort of Ancient Times

In the soft cushion of a flower
The eye of the answer-less god
Becalms the oceans in sequence
Measured to incremental moons
Distributing grace over silence.
We all are bound by innocence
Sacred in our union of humanity.
The god left the cow and the eagle
To overcome our loneliness.
When the bird sits upon a shadow
It is our hearts shaded to virtuosity.
And we listen below the blue air
To our memories collected twice
Within the comfort of ancient times.

Poems Modeled After Muso Soseki 1275 to 1351

Poems Modeled After Muso Soseki 1275 to 1351
Japanese Zen master, calligraphist, poet and garden designer.
Soseki wrote in short five or six line simple poems
describing people and places in his life in plain speaking terms.
This is a short exercise.

Religions

Five hundred fifty five ways to see god
I give a penny for each, they take back two
The dealer sweeps my bets off the table
And I walk away swearing never to come back

Self-Perception

I am never what I believe I want to be
Because I fall short in every area
I sleep on a precipice of acknowledgement
I wake with a blind eye toward my desires
Every time the mirror opens I turn away
And forget everything I know once more

A Poem of Nocturne

Between an alabaster moon and night
There is sweet nectar of music
Turning out the curfew of sounds
Into quiet peace by Chopin who
Left us to pray in his private world

She Who Died Little Known

Damned her and her primitive family
Who failed themselves and her in every way
Deserting her, abusing her, leaving her
To figure things out in her angelic way
That some god ignored and took her son
Took her life and health into a sinkhole
Where she forgot love and fought the pain
Until she forgot who she was under oxygen

A Poem of Redemption

Color me a traitor to crucifixion's promise
I believe only in a religion of fixing-things
To make amends by repetition of sorrows
A going over and over the same reading
Until the words take me into their meaning
And here you read me between grammar
As punctu ated, spell-checked and deleted

Love By Any Other Name is Lust

That eternal fascination women sizing up men.
Women waiting for the right man to size her up.
The lure of men to the fish hook.

Fallen eyes of lust,
giving over resistance to the tapping of a song
or the tripping over feet under a blurry eyed moon
 like lumbering hedgehogs come together unabashedly.
I remember Geraldine snugging into me darkly in the Dodge,
 radio playing Little Richard and the windshield wipers
keeping time with her heart.

I was Balboa the explorer searching with fear of her slapping me.
The world has an edge where we fall off into dizziness
forgetting right-from-wrong and we sizzle like steak-
on-a-grill for the thrill of blind fantasy of grope-and-hope,
that we incorrectly call love for shame of calling it otherwise.

God's Blessedness

Brash ostentatious slanted tongue acid word.
If you want laughter I will make myself heard.

It is easier for us to smudge out the past
For new memories are those that will last.

A sparrow cautions us or the hawks cry
Assures us that we live to never die.

False starts are the only way to supplant
Conversions of what day-dreams can't.

I no longer need to confess any misdeeds
Nor counter holding onto mistaken creeds.

Forsooth my face will tell you true
Of what my heart discovers new.

That "unbearable lightness" lifts me up
From one half full to one full cup.

And ages crimp me in gratefulness
As I welcome all of god's blessedness.

The Word

The word swelled out of its roots
And became a swoosh shot
Out of the boom of catastrophe

It stood outside of its echo
Stretched a lanyard length
Significantly spaced scant

In the beginning mayhem
reassembled cohesively
devolving itself intangibly
into super centrifugal
alignments like scoops
of bio chemical gas
waiting for ignition

Why Do We Need Poetry?

We all have our jobs.
We all have our egos.
Spaced between all our activities we relax.

Relaxing could be passive, i.e. media related
Relaxing could be active, i.e. using our hands to build or write.
Poetry is the one aspect of our lives that affirms human activity in
succinct terms - pointedly, concise, abrupt, serious, comical,
Poetry is a very thankfully short sermon,
after which we get on with our lives.
Poetry can be that short interjection between you
and a loved one that makes an observation.
Sit-com t v shows dialogue is usually comically poetic.

If you are on the phone with a friend
and you speak off-the-cuff that is poetic.
I love poetry because it is threshed down
to the bare essentials of language.

In play writing we were taught to make our characters
say their speaking part quickly and with no extra language.

Poetry is the skeleton of language.
It is the bare-bones of getting a point across.
My very first poem in college class that the professor liked was:
"He sits next to me in the car, driving,
wondering if he brought the safes."
Carl Sandburg wrote a beautiful poem,
"The fog comes in on cats feet."

In terms of human activity poetry
is the one aspect of living that we cannot be without.
We can get along without novels, plays, essays,
but we absolutely cannot get along without poetry.

I like poetry because it opens the pathways in my brain quickly
and keeps me clear thinking.
Poetry is important because it fulfills the hope
we all have that someone has a grip on reality
that is closer to the truth.

We wish for others to help us know
who we are and what is going on around us.
If someone says to us:
"If you eat green bananas you will turn green."
 We test this poetic quip by eating ripe bananas.
Poetry, if we write it or read it,
makes us hope for someone to be more sensitive
and kind, hopefully.

"He is a poetic soul."
is how I have heard someone referred to,
and it could be a nice way of saying,
"He is a pathetic soul. He needs to get on with life."
We never hear someone described as a, "Novelist-tic soul."
We could say,
"He is so long winded,
you never can tell if he is a poet or a narrative scribe.
Silliness. If you read this it is silliness and thank you

Michael Thomas

It is Last Call

It is last call.
The haves seen through smokey filtered restaurant windows,
warm in candlelight of amber comfort.
The have-not peek into a world of abundance.
Some where there is an end to the gifts of favor.
Outside the magical sense of privacy,
there is a ghost of deprivation waiting to invade the rich.
It is as inevitable as a machine grinding to a purpose.
We sit and beneath the stillness grows
 an insistent rumbling of discontent.
I fondle you with measures of my eyes.

I sooth you with words of affection
and blind you to the coming crisis.
We both will be caught in the time of famish.
We will be lined up and shot and thrown into a ditch
of lime covered injustice.
There will be no prayers for the dead,
only a sad silence as the smell rises noxious.

The simple fact of our memory
will be blotted out by time of terror / by time of destitution.
Rain will be our brother washing us bit-by-bit
and erasing al l indications of our once life.
Oh! My mother serenade me with your sadness.
Call to me in my sorrow and lift me up to your eyes.
I am a pilgrim of the horror of unkindness.
I am a burden to the light. I am the dark innocence of betrayal
by the obsidian powers of indifference.
Hail to the new order of importance.
Let there be no indication of my once-held affection for you.
Bow to the wrench-of-grunge. Kneel to the sanctimonious scourge.
The air is thin with the smell of blood and there is no room for white
lace between the curtains of hell holding in the acrid smoke
of bonfires in distances.
It is last call. Prostrate thyself atop the ashes of envy. It is last call

My Entry

Ju ju beans in the box
Holes in your socks
Holes in your head
When someone knocks

If you protest and throw rocks
We will put you in jail
And throw away the keys
For all the locks

Please judge my poem honestly
and do not dis me or kiss me or miss me
If I lose your contest,
then I will count my chickens as a just reward.

Just remember, I am a person of discrimination
From the Navajo Indian reservation
And I express my disjunctive elation
By climbing atop my 56 Chevy Impala in celebration
And screaming.

Jabber

"when you come to a fork in the road, take it."
it is always when i feel small that i am the largest.
a coin in my hand burns a hole in my pocket.
I left my first wife for cause and remarried her for no reason.
If we drive too fast, traffic will always slow us down.
my heart is on my sleeve. my head is in the clouds.
before life has any meaning there has to be much confusion.
marriage is an exercise in individualism.
where is your husband, Jesus said. he is in front of the t v.
give me flowers and i will give you a forest.
give me nothing and I will give you a ride out of here.
if you do not understand my poetry you are one step ahead of me
donuts for a dollar - leash and a collar - makes me want to holler
come to me for wisdom, all I can give you is ignorance
a person is famous around the world but not at home
my mother: "why do I have to love you? you're my son"
my dad: "relationships will be that way"
my mother to my dad: "if you think retirement is you touching me all
day, then get the hell out of the house and get a job."
I duplicate my feelings so as to reduce my anxieties.
I eat all I want and let my belly speak for itself.
I speak many languages but prefer silence.
I stand before my god with all my angels to defend me.
I am smart so that I can be dumb.
I am dumb so that no one can accuse me of being smart.
I am so full of it that often I need to talk too much.
Mark Twain: "Heaven for the climate, Hell for the conversation"
It is the sorrow and disappointment in life that gives life meaning.
Before you judge me, judge yourself.

Latest Poetry Books of Interest

I am a CPA and a writer.
I have been writing all my life with an English Major from college.
The attainment I reach for is predicated upon
all information coming to me.
The latest books of poetry stack up and I read them slowly.

Here are some of them:
Charles Bukowski - *On Cats* - My review:
Very well done with his sharp wit
Jeannie E Roberts - *Beyond Bulrush*:
Modern poetry in superior content
Muso Soseki - *Sun At Midnight*:
Succinct poetry in simple understand-ability
C D Wright - Several books of her narrative style poetry
of superior content
Anthology - *Faith & Doubt is a hodgepodge of lovely poems (2007)*
Sarah Howe - *Loop of Jade*: Best Selling straight-up poems excellent
Anthology - *Best Poems on the Underground*: One of my favorite discoveries of some of the best poems worldwide that I have ever read. This book is worth buying with short poems of amazing depth. It is the kind of book you can turn to and find something interesting ever time. (2009)

Thank you

Poem Of Emotion

Tiny invisibility.
A smallness of you sweetened by fantasy.
Tucked into crevices of my memory.
You don't even know you are there.
Going on with your mundane existence
far outside my sacred spaces.
Yesterday we collided like meteors.
Today you forgot me and I remember you
like some distant light measured by centimeters.
Your youthful sinews smooth inseams,
those graphical hips of grace I traced.
How I described your breasts.
How I made your lips come alive by contact.
All gone, disappeared into my loneliness.
The infinitesimal instant of tomorrow has
become whimsy lost within my heaviness of heart.

A Short Snippet Of My Father, Mike Ferris Michael Thomas

It was winter. Dad was in the front seat. Ma needed something from the grocery store. I let her off at the front door and parked out of traffic. My father was a person of few words. I used to attribute it to his lack of schooling. He worked all his life keeping his family of nine fed. I assumed he was asleep leaning against the car window. People were passing huddled over from the weather.
"Look at that one. A real love machine."
"Dad! I thought you were asleep."
"I thought you were asleep.
Did you see the ass on that one ?"
When my dad could no longer take care of himself, I used to give him his bath. I commented to him, "Dad where the hell did you get such a big penis? He laughed and told me to be grateful that he used it to give me life.
Maybe Telemachus washed his old weak father Odysseus and asked him the same thing. Or, If Ernest Hemingway had a son to help him over old age, he would have avoided suicide. Who knows? Here was my dad needing a wheel chair and stretching past age eight five and still consumed by sex. A man who was still "well endowed". I guess sex stays with us till the end. Maybe men who are misogynist get their penis measured at the last judgment.

An Essay On Death by Michael Thomas

When we die, we immediately are enclosed within a "space coma" to protect our psyche. "Watcher" spirits have been assigned to us. There are seven watcher spirits, as our group, who tend to us or heal us as we sleep in our temporary coma. Depending upon our consciousness level, we wake when it is appropriate for us.

Upon waking, we are told our situation and are allowed to proceed with what we chose for our next lesson. The guides or watchers give us advice but, within parameters, we can mostly do what we want. For instance, most people want to visit their funeral, which, like all reality, exists within the space/time bubble accessible to us as if it is happening when we desire it to become available to us.

Souls who have committed suicide will be allowed to sleep for long periods of time to overcome the self-abnegation or low self-image they generated. When these souls are finally rested, they usually have to be reborn into the very same circumstances of their suicide so that they can face and overcome the issues that led to their past suicide.

Souls that have a special interest that they wish to continue to pursue, will be allowed to be reborn into the general area of their fascination. For example, engineers, musicians, mathematicians, etc, will be allowed to find birthing groups that agree to take them into their families.

Souls that are inclined to be thieves will gravitate to groups with the same interest for them to be born successfully within that type of mindset.

One of the most accessible platforms for souls to be reborn are usually their ongoing family associations since these soul interact and know each other over long periods of time. This element of groups is paraphrased sometime as: "Like Kind Attract Each Other". Just as, on this face book site on the internet, the people we find most interesting are the ones who we find akin to, usually.

The most pertinent aspect of death is that we do not need to know what our past lives are because, as we are reborn, we must be free to develop a new life geared to our predisposition. It would be disconcerting for us to have the memory of our past obsessions interfering with our current goals.

The ongoing element of why we are souls and what our overriding purpose is in eternity is fodder for another short essay, later.

Waiting

We are accustomed to loneliness
Like the lion who sleeps hungry
Or stars emptied of adoration.

The moon sometimes forgets
And an orange dreams in red.

We walked this path before
along familiar foliage where
Our hearts were introduced
To joy that renewed us.

Late night reverie completed
The cycle of remembrance.
Our golden-eyed savors
Surrendered themselves to sleep.

Here, behind the veil, we lie dulled
Of glamour or inventiveness.
We are simply enervated shadows.

Here we await wakefulness for
Some new affections of love.

Note to a Fellow Poet

nothing but the color in your eyes
more blue than oceans of surprise
clear like a distant star pathway
linking me to your soul inner way

it's the only little joy I want to carry
into dreary hallways of my existence
where doubt collects like dusty balls
of shadowed insecurities we all have

tomorrow those doors will open
with a wink - with a glance
letting in light through veils
of stillness to measured
slow drum guitar solo
overriding emptiness

God Who Saw God Inside Himself

Life is a bottle of wine
opened at just the right time
when wisdom dictates silence
and those around us recognize
that we have much to say if prodded.

The looks on the faces we meet in passing
become indifferent to us and we grant them kindness.

The bean-brains who rush around us will arrive late for life.
The shallow-water people will never have enough to swim in.
The impatient people that we let pass in front of us
will want more space.

Life is a condition of reconciliation.
We give forgiveness for our fervent dramas.
We understand that we and all those, we meet,
will arrive together
inside a peaceful garden fenced around by angels
who stand like trees.
We will have benches beneath arbors to sit and like
Swami Vivekananda,
let go of passion's-desire and become God
who saw God inside himself.

My Prayer

Awoken from sleep faint forgetfulness
Open-eyed remembering gratefulness
For all gifts of sense-full consciousness
Good health enclosed by blessedness

I collect those points of last realities
Important tasks of all sizable duties
Memos, messages, books of entries
Wills, wishes of precious memories

Dear Lord I pledge my attentions
For client, friend whose mentions
I put forth as gifts of all intentions
As loving words of benedictions

I am not too proud but less inclined
Raise my thoughts higher of mind
Loosen sorrow, let patience unwind
Circle me in a spiritual light to bind

I profess no wisdom but ask grace
A ledge to grasp visions of a place
Where air is sweet, tongue to taste
Dark thoughts dissolve, pain erase

I am your servant of no hesitation
Ask and I will but rush to hasten
Myself for any job of any duration
I pray for all of high or low sta tion

Michael Thomas

Friday Night

Work ended.
Relax with a new recipe:
"Pork loin roulade with arugula pesto"
My cat, Percy, watches me cook from his perch
in the living room overlooking the kitchen.
He is indifferent.

Arugula pesto is made in the small food processor
with the twin blades spinning on the bottom.
I use tripe the garlic cloves and triple the pine nuts
as well as triple Romano cheese.

It grinds up to a lovely smell with the arugula leaves.
I remember Greg Penny, who made pesto ever day
in his restaurant where I was a waiter.
Penny had a twitch to his head
that made it nervous to watch him jerk constantly.
He was a good cook and the first time he cheated me on my pay,
I took my money out of the cash register each night
because I did not trust him.

Penny's pesto was the normal "Genoa" pesto of basil,
garlic, Romano cheese, pine nuts and parsley.
My pesto included the arugula leaves in place of the parsley.
Getting the pork splayed or butterflied and laid out flat was fun.
It took much pounding to flatten the pork out sufficiently thin.

My recipe called for less pork except you do not have much choice
in the store but to buy a large pork loin,
In the end I ended up with four lovely strips of pork
wound around the pesto filling.
I feel guilty, as a bachelor, cooking such a lovely meal
and yet not having a partner or woman to share it with.
But, I have been alone for all my life and I am much happier having
total freedom to do what I want always.

I learned long ago that my role
is to serve people through my accounting
and live a life of privacy.

For those who care, my sun sign is in
the twelfth house of the Babylonian astrological chart
that is used exclusively for the discipline.
I used to do astrological charts by hand years ago.
They are much easier on the computer now days.
Any ways, the twelfth house is the house of privacy
which categorizes me the way I live - alone.

So, on a Friday night I have four lovely rolled up pork loins
that I string tied to keep them cooking intact.
I probably will take three of them to the firemen in Canton
who enjoy many of the meals I cook
when I can get the food to them.

Firemen seem to enjoy food better than the Police of Canton.
I think there is an enjoyment firemen have eating
and cooking since they are in the firehouse so much
waiting for fires and they have time on their hands to cook.
So, enough of this boring detail. Thank you for listening to me jabber
and now I have to leave and eat one of my pork tasty dishes.

A Soul Embedded Night

reserved I lay myself thin over night's embrace
Woven into sadness
Laced by joy
Interlocked
Stitched

The lotus of my heart
resting on lily pads
buoyed affections
suspended
in silence

If there is a god
It is restful

If there is a spirit
I can trust it

I am a circle of
revolving love

There is no reason for the stars to envy me
And they dance in a tableau
Beside my quiet emptiness
Of a soul embedded night

Floating

Tomorrow laid itself in bones beneath stone memories.
I walk sideways to keep from running into doorways
that let in too much sadness.

Sometimes my patience is too short to clear the air
from dust of halos dissolved in trying to be safe.

I've been a loner.
I've held to a string loosened
in the wind of howling love.

Out there is doubt.
In here I'm hidden.

Your eyes burned me out.
Your indifference was
how you showed me
what was won or lost
without my choice.

I've been so alone
without a post or place to tie me down.

I would trade all the days of searching
for one parting heart of stone floating.

Morning/Evening Dove – Sing Thy Ancient Days

Hell holds still in silence as thy cooing
draws forth the tears of regretful souls
who, upon hearing you, die over again
in terrible sorrow for thy sound to cure
all the misshapen deeds and crimes
that clothe them insufficiently from fire.

Straight up from circled space comes
that cool sound of your pliant song
embroider of a tapestry of casements
falling forth thy fruits upon the star sky.

Oh! Dove of mystery quieted by joy
you send a fragrance over dull land
refreshing each crevice from staleness.

Oh! My dove of youth heralding entry
into the world of layers secreted below
all frivolous realities becoming unmasked.

Here upon the fair land your voice is heard.

Heard over the last summer days of faint
heart, you spur the hush-and-heavy hearts
to welcome new breath into their lungs.

My dove remembered over the walls of Troy
where echoes of defeat get buried beneath
thy sweet airs. Where tears dry into stones
of the dead warriors who leave the dust
of their lives mixed into the ashes of winds.

Here where Rome fell apart like a well-worn cloak.

Here where Constantinople warmed to the entry
of turban soldiers of the Shah marched in unison
over roads-of-Christianity, renamed for Mohammad.

Over the fears of all pilgrims coming together below
the throat-ed whisper of your magic dove calls.

Am I young?

Am I old?

I am forever for your voice, my dove.

I am beside myself in solitude to listen
at night and at morning time, to you forever.

In Fortunes Fame

In fortunes fame
When love is light
Hearts are feathers
Eyes are bright

We greet a morning
Like light was new
The soft dawn spilling
From skies of blue

Oh! That our troubles
Cease to exist
Our bones are brick
Our muscles thick

The last of doubt
We stand up straight
A cry goes out
We cannot wait

For crowds of angels
Release their airs
Above the darkness
Where there's no cares

To Her

My life
Memories
Traded for wealth
Forsaking fame
When giving up precious possessions
How the surprise from your eyes raised me past myself

Eternity is emotion
Of when the world slips away
And I cannot hold onto who I am

Renewal by forgetting
Becoming a delight by emptying all thought

Familiarity is the complacency
Of not being side-tracked

My heart is empty for your heart
To invade my darkness with light

Your ancient arms
Your musk nakedness
Sliding me away into oblivion
Forgotten heaviness that became a wisp
That was your memory I keep forever

I am Happy With Myself

First rule is: Take what you want without getting caught.
Second: Give back to the world all you have taken.

Universal rule: You cannot get what you refuse to give up.
I gave up marriage forty five years ago
and I have been given forty five years of bliss.

I watch married couples as if one is clinging to the other
as if one is bittersweet or mistletoe growing around the other.

Young married people are like new cottages
set inside white picket fences.
Old married people are like Halloween ghostly cobweb houses
set inside macabre scenes.

If you can get an ounce of sense from married people,
you can get bushels of wisdom from widows.

Society has set up marriage so as to avoid peoples fighting over sex.
Now, sex is evolution progressing. Without sex we have no continuity.
Sex puts people to sleep to keep them off the street.
Sex is the opiate of the masses. Sex is the mechanics of fantasy.
C lose your eyes and you can have sex with a tree,
then fall asleep under the wavering branches.
Even big ass people who hang over themselves in bubbling flesh,
think of themselves as sexy.

Sex is the underlying assumption of all human activity.
If we could read the thoughts of interaction,
we would be amazed at the hidden subterfuge.
We are barraged with sex starting with Adam and Eve
establishing the perimeters of fiction forever.

My mother told my father: "If you think retirement is having sex
with me whenever you want, all day long, you are crazy.
Get the hell out of the house. Get another job."
He did, in order to save his marriage.

I speak to every person in platitudes but envision myself deranged.
If one believes themselves as nuts, they come close to normalcy.
If one believes themselves as normal, they are truly nuts.

Mental institutions are full of mentally fit people
who are at rest with themselves.

If you want to judge a person, scrutinize their ambiance.
Stupid people look stupid and visa-versa.

It is the rare person who defers.
It is the normal person who is anxious.

Open the door for people so they get shot first.

Save yourself the trouble of being first in line
when there is no more money left in the bank.

I have much money in my accounts because I leave it alone.
Money likes to accumulate itself in silence.

The rabble of discontent emits from the refund lines.
People make themselves unhappy by their regrets.
I make ten reasons to keep what I have carefully chosen,
and therefore, no reasons to refund it.

For ten thousand years Buddha slept under the tree.
He woke and took a piss on the roots and the tree ate him.
God laughed.

I am happy with myself and assume others will, then,
leave me alone to be so.

"Something"

My father was a simple man.
No pretensions.
No assumptions of superiority.
A gentleness clothing him in charity and light.
The only thing he ever read was his readers digest copies
that stacked themselves unevenly on the shelf in the garage
near the folding chair where he sat and smoked a cigar
beside the open sliding door near the back of the car
where he used the chrome bumper of the Chevrolet
as a footrest while his miniature radio played AM stations
of tear jerking country music mixed in with the static
till his batteries wore down.

I often thought of my dad as Bootes, the constellation Urania's
Mirror. The relation to the farmer or herdsman with the fourth
brightest star in the sky, Arcturus, fits my dad perfectly.
In his youth, before he married my mother,
my dad was Bacchus or the god Dionysus of drink and revelry.
My mother made him swear off of gambling and alcohol.

Of all the aspects of my father that made him special to me,
was how he slept his life away. He was a very fat man,
portly with a big big belly.

He slept on the old couch in the living room
where I would jump on him and tickle him till he cried
"uncle". I would rub my stubble beard into his chin
till he howled like a bear.

My mother's efforts to intervene
and pull me off of him were never successful.
This episode of craziness would disrupt the whole family
watching television until dinner was served.

There was a hugeness of my father
that intimately connected me to his winter gloves.
In the hallway where the pair of leather gloves lay
puffed up as if his fingers were still inside of them:
I would heft them, smell them,
feel their animation as if he still had them on.

Eventually I would put my hands into the gloves
and feel the power of his strength with my hands
dwarfed inside their warmth.

Everything about my dad was related to his strength.
He had power in his legs and arms that could cinch me
if I ever let him get hold of me.
Years passed till he became helpless
and I would shower him and dress him.

I was in awe of his muscles
and used to love feeling them
in those intimate moments.
I never degraded him for his lack of education
or his ignorance of academic references.
If I told him a story of ancient melodramas,
he would listen raptly.

When I finished, all he would say was:
"Ain't that something."
He was "something" that I adored.

A Short Story

Grandpa got a tattoo.

Among the tattooed artists, he looked like a cream-sickle.
White-boy. Cracker.

They said: "How ya doing?"
He thought: (What the hell is Hank Williams twanging on the loud speakers, for? You would think "Adele" or "U2") He looked around and could not tell the whites from the blacks underneath all the tattoos. And then, the song went to Garth Brooks.

"Hi, I am Nicky. How can we help you?"
"Tracy referred me to Jason, for a tattoo."
"I will tell Jason. What's your name?"
"My grandchildren call me grandpa."

She smiles and the room goes loud with voices.
Grandpa looks around.
The cubicle to his right has an artist working on the arm of woman with her boyfriend standing watch.

"Hey! Want to see her tattoo?"

Grandpa moves slightly into the room and looks down at her arm. The whole underside is a bouquet-in-progress. She will have it hidden as she gets old and goes to a nursing home.

"I am going to ask Jason for a circle tattoo, right here."

Grandpa holds up his empty wrist and points to the veins.
They all nod their heads.
Jason is a small thin man with a partial bald head.

"Are you Grandpa?"

Grandpa says yes.

Jason holds up a paper and says: "I got your email
and here is what I drew."

The Circle-Of-Life, that Grandpa found, pops open on the held up paper.

Grandpa nods and says: "Yea! That's it. It looks nice. But, it is too large."

Jason shakes the paper and disappears back into his cubicle.
Grandpa moves back to the counter smiling at the faces facing him.

Five minutes.

Jason comes out holding up a smaller Circle-Of-Life.

Grandpa: "Perfect."
Jason: "Come back into my room."
Nicky: "I will bring him back."
Grandpa: "Do you want me laying down?"
Jason: "Whatever you want."

Grandpa talks a lot. Jason traces the image onto Grandpa's wrist, gets
Grandpa's approval and the buzzing starts tickling Grandpa's wrist.
We all want to be special in our insignificant lives. We will all become
wrinkled with saggy skin.

Well here it is. The wrist tingles. There is no turning back. A tattoo
forever on Grandpa's wrist. That great moment of decision is gone and
Grandpa holds his wrist for Jason to take a camera shot for his portfolio.
Grandpa: "It is beautiful. The Circle-Of-Life, just as I imagined it.......But,
it looks like a toilet seat." The room goes to laughter.
Here is Grandpa: "Well, if people give me shit,
I can turn my wrist to them."

Bigger and Better

Little bubbles of thought
Thinking makes its own space
Divided among so many other
Children's wand circles bursting

Little big-bangs breaking
Inventing entropy
Changing a life into a memory

Oh! I knew there was something more
Than copulation when a monkey went to school
Eating bananas out of decoupage lunch boxes

And the firemen's eyes enjoyed the fire-down-to-ash

When Joe, the welder, slipped the mask down
Butane blue cut a path through steel
Like the way he carved the turkey
Or surgically cut his wrists to leave us

I guess spit becomes a harvest of oceans
Or when we piss into the wind-of-wetness

Gloria felt herself becoming a vapor
In a slide-show-of-screams as he woke her by injections

Take as prescribed a dose of energy twice daily
It is exponential and a serious expansion of brain cells

Dinosaur pea-brains bespeak their weight-in-words
If a rattler bites you, X the spot and suck before the venom expands

I got nothing against Ebonics

Like "Ma mouth got a full of your shit, mother fucker,
And I'm giving it back to you with my foot."

Energy displacement of the priest fucking altar boys
And somewhere there is a snake-in-the-woodpile
Biting the Pope right in his "ex cathedra" ass

The hurts others cause us
Become energized angers

I leave, but I shall return
bigger and better than ever

When Everything is Balanced

When everything is balanced
We watch for anomalies
To come out of the blue
And disrupt us

In the army it was called
Preventive maintenance

In civilian life it is called:
Waiting for the shoe to fall

Either way, it is called
"The only thing constant
On the face of the earth
Is change."

There are certain ways to understanding balance
Maybe we will call those ways: "cautiousness"
We caution ourselves that: No matter
How wise or smart we are, there is
always more wisdom or smarts
coming at us, down the road

That son-of-a--bitch
Who cuts us off, is
Us at another
Time & place

The one thing we hate
Is to begin to have feelings
For that ex-spouse who we left

Maybe he-or-she had some good points
That we can find in the "bagger" at the checkout counter

Money Blues

Gonna tell you when I get a dollar in my pocket
My pocket gets bad news and gets empty like a rocket

They standing in line with their hands out
I close my eyes and want to cry or shout

Gonna tell you when I get a few bucks
The green dollars peel away like corn shucks

I got a girl sitting easy in her chair
She got a sister who got blue hair
When I give her my paycheck
Her sister gets a tattoo on her neck

I feel like a fish with no water to breathe
Like a rooster who sleeps till morning leaves
Like a silver snake with no color up my sleeves
Like a preacher who got no sermon I believe

My sister and brother owe me a king's ransom
My ex-wife tells me that I am handsome
But they all whispering that I am old fashion
Cause they want all my stocks to cash in

Travelling

I travel in the land of words
The kind that spin both ends of my tail
With the vowels of winds suspending ears to spiraled tree trunks
Oh! The hunger of wolfs embracing syntax with teeth blooded,
with eyes speared to bone bristle

Catch the movement of creatures between the foliage of forever

See the scurry of syllables limb-to-limb of chickadees
entangled by dizziness

We left the twisted bows beneath the bowers of bereavement –
sweet was the release of sorrow for our wisteria loved ones

Angels wandered with shore birds rising out of the muck of mucilage

I was beached with caregivers trying to coach me back to the ocean
My blow holes silent in a partial death of whale musicality entombed
out-in-the-open with an un-entwined Gulliver restraint

Co co co spelled the dove

Achoo abruptly - and my heart stopped for the verbs of velocity –
see, I was the hawk of hovering hang-glide –
upside-down and in-and-out abounding daredevil
of pirouetted gravity remembering only the twisted ends
of de-railed rainbows

This was my behest to humanity - my spirit seed of vitality risen out of
the moist spring earth of skunk cabbage and three leaf trillium laced
inside of the pensive scab-bag dog tooth violets spotted pointed leaves
whispering to Virginia blue bells nourished nonsensical

Happy Spring/Easter

To all of you who remain clients, friends and associates.
I thank you.
My message is forbearance.
As Job learned - nothing is permanent - only gratefulness.
All stories come to an end.
All stories start over again.
The only thing constant on the earth is change.
I am the biggest fool in the world
and when I think I am wise is when I have become
a bigger fool.
The one thing I have in my life
is being thankful for you and all the comforts I have.
If it is taken away, I will sit at the gates of the city in rags
and be patient for whatever comes next.
Thank you and happy spring/Easter

Letter to Adam

I wish I could refer William Bates to you for painting or any miscellaneous jobs you may have connected with your advancing new home or any of yours or your mother's properties.

At the start of him helping me, there was an oil leak from his truck that caused the Canton authorities to elicit the Environmental Protection Agency. The EPA resisted, at first, then gave in to naming my driveway a major catastrophe. For weeks, volunteers helped squirrels wash off grease. They came from working in Puget Sound on the U S S Valdez oil spill and sang folk songs and ate half sandwiches of hummus with whole wheat pita bread.

If polluting my driveway was the only thing I can relay to you about William, it might end there against his favor, but please listen.

The small job of repairing a section of wall around my skylight expanded itself into the whole north wall and now includes the common wall between my neighbor and myself. William said that his efforts to replace the drywall, needed extensive work that did not meet the eye at first sight. Whole families of various birds now have built their nests where the roof shingles were never replaced.

To boot, I will need to replace the wall-to-wall carpet in the whole house from him tracking oil from my driveway on the bottom of his shoes. I am sure that he meant no harm in leaving his footprints everywhere. And, I have called in Maize and Blue to paint over the streaks and bumps after the wall and ceiling are fixed. Maize and Blue specified that they had never seen such a mess. They took pictures for their website calling Bill's work a memorable mess and titled the series of pictures: "Don't let this happen to you." As well as rectifying the overflowed toilet and area that leaked down into Ginger's living room below me.

I truly wish I could highly recommend William, but, if you do try to use him, be sure to fill your refrigerator full of food, as mine is now completely empty. He took the caution to leave all his empty cans and wrappers on the floor or in the drawers where my silverware used to be.

He presented me with a bill for over fourteen thousand and said he would be happy with a discount if I lit a candle for his grandmother who is sick in hospice in Valenzuela.

I know you to be a charitable and kind man. But I fear that you might have to contact my therapist, Barbara Jean Sullivan, if you use William. She will give you the same answers for depression that she gave me: "Put your head between your legs and kiss your ass goodbye." I am going to be finished paying off William for his work in the year 2045 and my family will complete this debt when my grandchildren's children reach the last of their lives.

Parts of Me

parts of me you will never know
how I sleep
how I relieve
what I believe
don't want any inquisition
keeping secret about my position
on birth control
on what god has the right mojo
my parents never told me
how they loved to have me
I prefer to think I came in a capsule
all the little boys down the alley in Detroit
charged to show their dicks to us smaller boys
now, I wish I had not wasted my twenty five cents
she gave me two children
I stayed home to tend to her after each kid
it was a time of concern for her comfort
I never told the divorce judge
he was quick to get us out of the way
so he could go back to his chambers
parts of my heart I keep from you
I will give you a hint
you will not find me on the streets-of-regret
because all that shit that went down the toilet
is a part of me the department-of-life will filter and file away

The Horse Snorts

when the rain comes
sleep follows it
patter roof sidewalk
earth leaves you softly

when you wake, later
a refreshing silence
reminding us rain has left

we return to sleep
in the emptiness of its echo

we are city folk
and the smell of rain
or the streaks upon our windows
or the glisten of grass aftermath
is like a cowboy's saddle
left over creases from age

we have never mounted
spurred the horse on into damp trails
left by the departed thunderstorm
but the horse remembers and snorts

Michael Thomas

Hope

Some bow their heads like shore birds - cranes
pecking into the mirror of spirituality
with shimmering blurriness of
a fish motionless
silver currents
of secrets

Some sky write their insistence
into banners of faith that
never take no for an
answer dissolving

I listen to time worn shadows
of saints situated
in a hierarchy
of heaven

Here is the best we can draw out of the chaos:
Someone took advantage of us
giving us a real hope
in forgiveness

Tears

She walks bent slightly
Carrying onion sheaves
In faded bags

Shadows scrunched in scarves
Follow her on cold morning mists

Those sturdy peasant legs
Keep her straight up in tennis shoes

We know the color of mucilage skin
Tattooed by field dust sun shine

An ancient herald banner waves invisible
Over the silent sadness of her years ago
When her dreams soaked out of her sweat
And her eyes crossed deserts behind sand blindness

Little girl grandmother city market madness
Fresh vegetables for withered hands
Feel the veins of lettuce
Test the tomatoes

Pass back the full bags
She presses forward
Among crowded
Indifference

Time skips
Blister tears
Tear inside me

Oceans Erase Me

I will let you know when I have had enough
full to the scuppers
bloated
bam bam wamma dam

drink the ocean
eye the sky till I die
stride past horizons
Cyclops into infinity

her love made me small
screwed into the socket of her
bolt-nut frozen piston in her chamber
she took me up out of the well when she needed water

God shot the bullet of sorrow into my breast
smoking gun target of tenderness
I face life Swiss cheese
remember the perforated steel planking roofs that made streams of sunlight fall over the silence of our hooch's or living spaces in Vietnam. When the mortar rounds hit the roof, they spread shrapnel over the sleeping bodies of McCarther and all the ghosts who bled blue.

We were blessed by the hail of bullet holes opening up the blue sky inside the C-130 flying boxcars and Zachie sat on steel sheets in the swivel belly-turret of the flying fortress and he came home after fifty flights of shooting up the German sky full of ack-ack machine gun bullets. He came home and was forgotten. He had three kids and a wife to watch him fade into oblivion.

Gotcha by the balls
Hail to the conquering hero
Saved the world from hell's face

I will let you know when it is all over
wait for my cue

We vomit the entrails of monsters.
We excrete the devil
Let loose the phlegm
Cough blood
Spit

All that is left is a shell of a soul of emptiness
and, then, I have had enough
to put me to sleep
stop me dead
in my tracks
stone sorrow (repeat)
till oceans erase me

Women versus Men (Tiresias)

Women need to learn their place below men in the hierarchy.
They are inferior to male thinking patterns.
Their place is to have babies and raise them.
They should cook, clean and arrange furniture.

I once was a woman and I served.
I never complained about my monthly period.
I would listen and not speak until spoken to.
I knew that I should never display my intelligence.
I sprayed myself with cologne and never ate till everyone was full.

I never went to college and secretly joined a school advertised on
a match book cover - I think it was called "School Of Attainment"

The world would be a lot more peaceful if women
just stepped back and let men rule it.

Men know how to conduct war.
They know how to display hate properly.
They have an uncanny sense of what words will offend women.
They have the ability to forget birthdays and anniversaries.
If you invite a man to a party, he will bring a candy bar that he buys
from the counter at the gas station.
Men know how to fart properly.
They know every possible story of inflated manhood
that has been told over and over for centuries.

Of course, the world may assemble itself into order through
the efforts of a women,
but it stays in place despite men's impertinence.

If you want to prove yourself as a woman,
invite a man to meet you behind the dumpster near Rite Aid
at midnight and tell him to flash his headlights.
I guarantee he will be there looking for you.

He will have a story ready for the police that he is not gay
and that his brother just got in town from duty in the mid-east.

A woman should open doors for a man and always let him make
an entrance ahead of her.
He is, of course, the stronger one to face any fuselage of bullets
before her.

When I was changed into a woman for seven years,
Apollo questioned me in full assembly of the gods
and asked me whether a man or woman
has the most fun in a relationship. I said to the god,
that women have the best fun and Zeus blinded me. Go figure.

Jesus Laughs

Jesus smiles
He knows Mel Gibson hates Jews
Looks into Hitler's kaleidoscope
Through looking glass of horrors
he wakes all the dead in both worlds

Jesus drank wine till the world disappeared
His mother was glad when he sobered up and laughed

We speak of gods in reverence
While Zeus pinned the tail on the donkey

Jesus told the crowd,
"Remember to keep holy what came before me"

There were tears
Jesus wiped the faces of sinners
He offered chewing gum to disbelievers
He reached into his robes and brought forth grace
Like silver spears of silence, his smile evoked awe

The apostles all agreed that Jesus was the real ticket
They never could figure out how the man grew past his roots

I will tell you what makes Jesus laugh:
The way the world saw and understood him,
made him break out in mirth

Life
Tin can flattened
Shaggy paper whisked windward
Left from love in thought of tomorrow

Life
Narrow focus
In a vast eternity

Life is that momentary joy
reached by awareness of beauty

Or sorrow - Often cloaked in reverie
of mischance or regret

Life is that snippet of multitudinous lives
that shape our soul

Visiting Gerhard & Martha Woltemade's Grave

Woodward and Eight Mile
Woodland Cemetery
Stone house entrance
Back left to corner

I always take a piss behind the solitary stones

Martha was a poetess of minor output
Gerhard was a product of German Trade
where he spent two years at each discipline
till he became a journey man
Electrician, Plumber, Tool and Die, Carpentry, Plaster Specialist.

He raised birds and tended tropical fish tanks.

When he finished his full life of hard work,
they buried him beside his wife.

I was his friend for seven years till he died.
When the funeral home was empty,
I raised his hands and felt the strength of his life flow into me.

This is where he is buried beneath a simple plaque
near trees in private.

Autumn Days

From my childhood I knew I was special.
Not in a way that I would announce,
But in a way that kept me above
The ordinary mundane things of life.

I exhibit kindness
Generosity
Love of nature
Belief in some special power or god.

The most prominent aspect I have
is my respect of the old and dying.

When I visit them near the end of their lives,
they cry that someone remembered them.
I smile inwardly knowing that not one soul will remember me
and it makes me laugh to think I am special
when the leaf of my life will blow into a pile of Autumn days.

Leaving You

You were not here to feel the cold.
April cannot let go of winter,
Like I try hard to let go of you.

The trees shiver in anticipation of change.
Little leaves left over on limbs, in tenacity, cannot let go.

Your death let go of me.
I never cried outwardly.
You never would have known either way.
They categorized you as crazy last three years.
I let you go because you abused me last three years.

Maybe you could not have helped yourself,
But, I do not care. You had time to help yourself.
Life let go of you.

Secretly I visited you at the night hospital.
I washed your sweat.
I folded your head back on the pillow.
You did not respond,
I loved you,
turned and
finally
left you
for spring.

Death

Hold pieces happiness dissolves
Fresh love soon turns inside-out
Furtive dogs awake hunger growls
Pain causes even saints to shout

Oh! How we clenched so furiously
First we found each touch a fire
And sleep overcame us drowsily
In dreams we conjure new desire

There's such truth to loneliness
When left alone we think on why
Our lips once sealed with kisses
Close silent to love's memory

Passion passing in parting clouds
Weaves itself into death shrouds

My Big Fat Tax Cake

Oh! My god in heaven
My big fat tax cake
Gluten free unleavened
Bake-n-shake
Seven-come-eleven

Clean up the counters
My best knife serrated
To dice all encounters
Slice cash decimated

Dependents exemptions
Five ounces of tears
401-K of deductions
No whiskey or beers

Money-less cabbage
Pennies of fears
Savings are radish
Profit disappears

Uncle Sam's in hell
Congress deranged
Stock values fell
Net worth rearranged

Mix oil vinegar
Saffron All-spice
Donate with care
Double the price

Lie and get caught
Bake in your jewels
Melt gold in the pot

Poverty in the pews
Our tempers are hot
No news is good news

It is late, I need sleep
No lunch for the kids
My pockets are deep
My budget's in the frig

The cake is finished
The cupboards bare
Turbo-Tax diminished
My net worth declare
Monopoly is spinach
Bankruptcy is here

Overcoming

That first
Match throat
Church cough
Like on a date snuffling - to be not embarrassed

It was a culture
Of differences
To swill or savor "Goebels"
That beer name fell into obscurity

Walking home
Waiting for relativity to come back
Vomiting as an aid
We matched our steps

You were so much wiser than all the others
And it was seasons later that I came to realize
There was no sense to insecurity and quaffing

With You Beside Me

before logarithm
or incision of icicles
collected fulcrums
leveraged laconic
love called loosely
absent intangibles
left over lassitude
lightness laughter

you were love pistachio
cu cu circumference
encircled cylindricals
all the alphabetical numerical bindings
in leather ledgers of mosaics

what can I say to insure you of my fidelity?
you will never leave my caravan
the desert likes you at midnight
the sun stretches your eyes
the heat calms your fears

here on top of Asia
bumped into clouds
I am your boondoggle

trust
lust
musk
every example
slides into infinity
with you beside me

Loving my Neighbor

Kim replaced her dog. "Cooper" was named after the car.
Coop is a yapper. Left outside to do his business,
he barks and complains.

I yell out the open screen on the second floor:
"Coop, we love you / Coop, hey Coop we love you."
He barks and barks. Kim yells up to me: "He's a nervous little one."
Kim only has her daughter and Coop fills her days
since her husband deserted.

Kim is a nice person. Her husband and her fought.
I never fully trusted the man.
He was a person who took advantage.
He was a quiet man.
Beneath his silence there was an unhappiness.

He created his own dissatisfaction with life. Kim was a good wife.
He did not like himself therefore he could not like Kim.

Coop barks because he is self-confident.
Kim's husband was self-insecure. He never barked.
Coop will stay faithful to Kim because dogs and pets
know how to express emotion and when they become your friend,
they never will disappoint.

Kim's husband has been gone for over three years
and his daughter plays with Coop in the back yard.
I can tell she misses her father.

What can we do when we see life unfolding right in front of us?
We let Coop know we love him and he barks less
and Kim and her daughter feel good that I like Coop
instead of being irritated over his nervousness.
Kim and her daughter need to feel good about themselves
and I do what little I can do in the situation.
It is my way of loving my neighbor as I would want to be loved.

Holes in my Head

it's what the mice do to the grain sacks
pharaoh says put the cats in the racks
aboard ship they find all the cracks
they never suffer scurvy or blacks
not to my idiocy or what it lacks
follow their footsteps or tracks

savagely, kids play ball-n-jacks
trading marbles pull-string packs

domineering duck quack quacks
solemn night loon moon backs

disturbed forest's lumberjacks
leave the fallen trees in stacks
float em down-river in packs
waste their pay on heart attacks

i favor maidservants on their backs
lovely rhythmic naked loin smacks
joy for what the hollering lacks
miscued comical gentle whacks

no praise or posted plaques
for poetry from poet hacks

Michael Thomas

Light Years Ago

They will carry weight of
their anger into the lightness
of afterlife in a sleepy haze.

The art of the soul
paints forgetfulness.

A supreme catalog
filed away for remembering
is what we call our dreams.

I feel the relief of their hatred
giving me joy of forgiving them.
It is like they float away in feathers.
They leave me in a flour wisp cloud
to where I even forget their names.

I balance my heart against their hatred.

The hardest part of leaving this world
is to evacuate the sniping to exhaustion.
Say good bye to deliberate denigration.
Open the chambers of elation to healing.
And those bitter energies of sadness will
see us as a star never knowing that we
are released from them into light years ago.

No Light

bird in me nests
open wounds heal
awaiting morning
restless

tomorrow is a new ocean
an unexplored castle on the Moors

we travel in our sleep
past boundaries
free of heaviness

as the huntsmen drink ale
the flash of a sword
reminds them of death

we remind ourselves
that no Samurai outlived his deeds

no light from our souls
is ever extinguished

before judges
we hold to truth

after passing into emptiness
we begin to rejuvenate
little spaces linked
as prayer beads
into eternity

Today, Ya Finest Lite

fa ya canna find answrs te lief been suc e fole
when lief finds ye actin so ye hae nae to rue
wee bit e thot wud du ye beter en da end
ei, ya wish fa som thing borrowd to lend

late do we all face misrie n paine
fa wit ot bad times we nae to gaine
n out a sorow comes wonder joy
fa ye need to climb high to ploy

me motha n me da both kept peace
together the gae lief long lease
paid they bills each silent slept
n never fa they needs they wept

how tomorow outshines itself so brite
en ye give today ya finest sparkle lite

Reflection

you are coal
undiscovered
nature's forgotten
as idylls of history
record events - you carry stone of a short lived past

it is neither love nor hate
it is a pebble on a rock infested shore line
where you lay un-differentiated by a dulled ego

your sullied sheer blandness
makes only importance to me:
that I guard against mimicry
and never mirror you by reflection

With You

I cover myself in gold shield
painted heart of amber
wished into an horizon
silenced by little winds
arrows of scintilla sorrow

come let me absorb the whispers
 of willow trees sowing
in a summer breeze

for season shifts between lulls
of temperate shadows
become invisible

there were many exact elements
configured within timeless seconds

above the cries of despair,
I quelled the hawk of heaven's hungers

before all changes I became all one
in the circle of life blessed

when you discover me
absent is when we shall
be together forever

Silence

I went along for the ride.
Sometimes the journey is murky.
You seemed to be what wishes were about
like an allurement that diminishes with time.

The headlong rush turns into a crash.
Lessons learned turn into realizations
that madness was always in you, coming
out with pressure of aging and ill health.

I cannot regret because I instigated.
We are less than perfect and level ourselves
by the bumps and bruises of love.

Come back to life.
The grave is too limiting.
Come back and speak to me of
rain tears running the eye shadow down.

Come here once more and face the truth
that your unresolved issues overwhelmed you.

I am waiting for some answers in the small space
that remains between me and silence.

Michael Thomas

Just Because

Just because
I want a new car
just because

I swear when I drop things
just because

I prefer being single
just because

Please do not bother me for having my house cleaned
I prefer having it done by someone else
just because

I drive slow
just because

I open the doors for people behind me
just because

I believe Jesus never died on a cross
so damn me to hell
just leave me alone

The Catholic Church is all wrong about abortion
I want abortion to be removed from the inferior medical situations and given a status in all hospitals so that any women who wants an abortion cannot fear getting ripped or having physical problems from less than standard operatives. What is the big deal, the world has an over-population problem,. as-it-is..

Get over your ego about abortion. The soul enters or leaves the embryo as it feels necessary to fulfill its reincarnation prerogatives.

I do not believe in heaven or hell.
 We simply come back and come back till we get it right.

let me be, please. leave me alone - just because

Existence as we Know It

Nature, in universality,
is a complexity of its own agenda.
Consciousness parallels nature,
working in conjunction.

Earth day is a rather self-indulgent
humanistic ego concept.
Any human who assumes superiority
on this earth fails to recognize
that the only thing constant in the universe is change.

All creation follows similar rules on any star system.
The spectrum analysis from light
coming from any planet or star
can be categorized so as to divulge
scientific principles governing all planets.
Atmosphere, water table,
mineral content and more,
can be determined by the Doppler Effect.

For me, earth day is every day.
I know that small gestures showing my appreciation
for an earth that gives me existence,
is rewarded in balance.

If I pick up a plastic container and recycle it,
there is the effect of
"better to light one candle than to curse the darkness."

I have an initial reaction of horror
at trash not being recycled properly.
And then I remember all the extinct civilizations
that went through
their cycle and exist no longer on the earth.
It is, as if, the earth swallowed them up.
Or, as if, the earth compacted the extinct
places and made them part of the earth's
composition or layers of sediment.

I have an imaginary test:
That if we did a core sample of the earth
from one pole to another pole,
we would see all the historical layers
of phases of earth life.

I extend this imaginary test out into the
universe and play-with-the-idea of doing
a core sample of space
from both ends of our galaxy
and analyze creation from this sample,
we would find star explosions
as well as star lives that follow nature's rules.

Earth day is a reminder
that earth has its day every day.
Earth day is a reminder
of the vast interacting network of events
and changes that make up this miraculous planet
we live on as small insignificant microscopic particles
collecting up into the whole of existence as we know it.

Michael Thomas

A Few Friends

Mozart is my friend.
He puts me to sleep.
Shostakovich preludes sing me up.

I stack the new books of poetry into my head
as I learn how others speak in words
 that become my excuse for partners-in-poetry.
The fair contests are held by members
that I catalog with promise.

For, going on ten years,
I have thanked those who read my poems.
I feel guilty that I do not read more,
here that are truly worthy. When I admire a writer,
I try to go out of my way to read their work. But,
for the most part, I am insulated and alone
but never lonely.
I want not for friends because my books
and poems are my comrades.

The pleasant sounding occasional
pop music is relatively minor to my listening. I prefer,
mostly, classical and my heart is healed
by the sounds of my favorites.
As the years go along,
I acquire admiration for the balance of words
 written as melodic poetry.
I mistrust the chat and irrelevancy of commonness.

The separate parts of my heart are kept
in thanks for quiet corners of writings that please me,
 and I thank you all who read and comment
as my few friends here on this site.

Women

Creature of humanity
Stood straight against a vociferous wind
Societies savior
Unfazed by gender confusion

She tends gardens of our hearts
Keeps order within mayhem
Opens her knees
Emitting the whirlwind infant cries
Subduing a bellicose insistence

Under covers of sensuality
Universal women linked
By endurance
Co-joined in tempers
We can only bow to the inscrutable
We can only give way to her persistence
We all rest easy by her efforts to show us
Love of orange,
blue diffusion as color effect upon our shadows

Unselfish Stories

I remember sitting restless in a stuffy church on Sunday listening to a sermon that was irrelevant to my life.

I remember the shifting bored parishioners all around me trying so hard to avoid eye contact and anxious for the ceremony of tediousness to end.

My thoughts went out to the sunlit park with my family spread out on picnic tables with food and the games awaiting on the soft summer grass dotted with blankets to lay on and fall asleep with our stomachs full of hot dogs, pork and beans, hamburgers and all the deserts of side dishes that were too numerous to fit into our imaginations.

To me, that picnic was the real church and this closet of prayer with a priest who was stupefied by an invisible god that never revealed himself, this house-of-holiness, was the fake church.

I imagined if Jesus ever was to come back to fulfill whatever his mandate was, he would be better off coming back to one of our picnics and joining in with a paper plate full of good tasting food. He would be better off laughing with Uncle Rocco shouting at his son at the end of the table. Better off with Aunt Thelma shoving more and more food into his dish without him even asking.

There was always a wistful sadness when the day ended and all of us pitched in to clean up the area, putting all the trash into green barrels that had bees and flies swarming around them.

My family was suffering from the effects of the end of World War Two. All my uncles had served and survived the quashing of Hitler and America saving the world from the Nazis. My family was celebrating our small place in history as the victors over evil. Was our society selfish? History was full of good people being killed and cities destroyed by armies of dis-concern. Marauders of ages past had burnt out and killed all peoples in conquered cities till all that remained was dust.

In retrospect, was our society self-indulgent and selfish over this superior attitude following the end of the war? Did all the sacrifices of soldiers dying on ill-remembered battlefields in Europe and Asia matter as a form of selfishness? We cannot surmise the full impact of history since we were too close to the event. A true learning lesson of life can only come long after the event takes place. It is if this: When we are immersed within life, we are too blind to see outside of life.

Did Jesus die on a cross as a form of selfishness? Or did Jesus go to India to study Buddhism. Did he watch as a zealot took the job on as the professed messiah to fulfill the prophecy of being the appointed one?

Did all the innocent civilians of Europe give their lives up as they fell within the range of bombs and bullets that were meant for the various soldier enemies of each other? Were those victims the un-selfish ones?

I dream of an example of a peaceful mother being pulled from her cottage home with soup on the stove and a table set for her f amily. I dream of her cat and dog being so mixed up over her abrupt absence. Her gardens wilting and dying from not being attended. I dream of her anguish as she is stripped, raped, thrown naked into a pit and shot and covered over with lime and dirt in the ignominious end to a life of curtailment. To me, she and all her families of a holocaust of madness, were the true people of selfishness. To those unknown unceremonious dead, I bow my head in thanks for their unselfish stories.

Prioritizing of our Information Age

We, all of us, are immersed
within an unimaginable store of information.
Years ago, I had the Detroit libraries
to fill my imagination
in an attempt to read every book
 I could get my hands on.

In my youth I had mailed to me the
"Congressional Record"
with all the discussions in both houses of congress.
The focus in the fifties and sixties
was what effect computers were going to have on our society –
be it detrimental or positive.

In high school Mrs. Virginia Ladendorf and Elinor McHarg
guided my reading and allowed me to work
in the library filing books.

At age fifteen, I moved in with my grandmother
and had stacks of books surrounding my bedroom.
To this day, despite the computer,
I still buy and read books and books.

In the early years of computers,
I was fortunate to have the first Pet Commodore computer.
Next came the IBM System/23
and the years of struggling with DOS change after change.

Finally we could buy stand up
and lap tops that exceeded our beliefs.
Now, in 2016, we can buy stand up or lap top computers
that only cost in the $300 range.

Apple or Microsoft computers now
have similarities
that have moved them to sufficient compatibility.
Now, we have information,

storage and conversion systems
that would astound our past generations.

All the books on shelves in libraries around
the world dealt with the paper deterioration
by converting these existent manuscripts
to microfilm and releasing all these books to the public,
almost all free.

It is unbelievable what we have access to with the internet.
 The first movable press produced the bible
 and the world shook with change
as that book allowed individual readers
to ascend to the ranks of facing off
with churches or organizations that once

held their only copies of books
as weapons to control peoples.

Now we have the ability to research topics
to the most fullest sense of their revelations.
 Civilizations rise and fall
mostly based upon over use of nature's gifts:
earth, water, sun and the dispersing of minerals
or information to exhaustion.

Buckminster Fuller postulated
that civilization would use up all fossil fuels –
then turn to using our sun to sustain us.
And, finally, in a futuristic sense,
use of all the suns in our galaxy to sustain us.
In an essay I read recently,
the author tried to bridge our use of information
with our ability to live compatibly with earth.
So, my essay is an attempt to bridge
our actions to our ideals.

My first stipulation is this:
We can never have enough information.
No matter what we can cram into our heads
or into our storage devices, we can never have enough.
The revisions and addendum's
 to our retrieval base is inexhaustible.

My second stipulation is this:
The information that we can relocate
or retrieve is always just enough
to solve the problem or quandary at hand.

My third stipulation is that
what we do not pull out of our available data,
is left there for us to access at some future life or time,
depending upon what our needs are at that time.

My fourth stipulation
is that the total data base
never gets destroyed,
despite what earth's evolution agenda plans
on an explosive scale
 because the information
does not reside totally on

tangible surfaces but exclusively within
the minds and consciousness of souls
who can rethink it any time needed.

My fifth stipulation is that the data is like flora
or creatures reproducing themselves
by specific laws no matter what planet arises
out of the realm of infinite possibility.

I have purposely stayed away from judging the people
who each have different views
and mannerisms of retrieving
and re-assembling their research
to give further enlightenment.

I do not care how ignorant
or how intelligent their research is.
Like a fire-person not questioning the morals
or character of their victims,
but simply saving them from a fire-death.
We have different peoples
and purposes for research
and assembling information
and these peoples natures are not important,
but only their depth of revealing something new
for us to chew on.

The Beast of Degeneracy

Little things about my neighbors. So irritating that they put their discards inside black bags for trash pickup. Bags of forever that get strewn over a hilly plot of land called a "dump". It is as if the township gives them the right to not recycle. The township collects their black bags once a week. Black bags full of glass, paper, plastic and the filmy rot of leftover food stuck to the insides of cartons or wrapped in paper bags from McDonald's or Wendy or some fast food restaurant that also smells of french fries being deep fried.

I cannot hate my neighbors but I evaluate them as very unaware. They do not discuss philosophy or history or art, literature or something of substance. They talk about the latest sports stories or movies or the weather.

We truly live in a vast wasteland and as time goes by, I fall deeper and deeper into T S Eliot's writing or Ezra Pound who drew the masses of peoples as inert or as empty-headed humanity.

Various Poems New

#1

Tomorrows dreams take hold
Within cotton clouds expanding over us unsuspecting

Little spaces of desire bubble up to the tops of our thoughts
Built up frustrations dissolve by friction –
our fingers wash clean by virtue

Our past hurts leave us exhaustively
The tell-tale sufferings of unkindness harden
and break off the veneer of our soul

Maybe right-from-wrong does not matter,
only that we did our best and continue to do so

Our clothed presence is our comfort
What comes undressed is our trust
That we try our best to avoid hurt

We cannot look for old avenues of absolution
For, in our innocence we will find a salvation of simplicity

Michael Thomas

When poetry came to me at an early age
I flubbed, hedged, spoke loud but without weight.

It took time to talk to the wind
To speak languages of the stone
And hear little secrets of oceans
To feel granules of an earth
between my fingers.

I forgot your eyes.
I do not know your weight.

Time is in my favor to discover
what will appear when I throw flour over you.
Poof!! You will fill in as I imagined
And I will breathe a sigh of relief
when I discover you and learn what is in your mind,
What is in your secret compartments
that I can hold fast too before my poetry runs out

#3

Touch me, I might crumble
Into Frosted Flakes like
Tony the tiger.

That's my dog, Tige.
He lives in the shoe.
My name's Buster Brown.
Look for me there too.

You are, Side Saddle Sally
I am Roy Rogers of your days.

Yippy Kay Yay
Yippy Ki Yo
Iim an old cowby
From Ko Ka Mo

Ilene, you melt the snows in my heart
The way country western songs start.

There is a prairie ranch home
With flies going in-and-out the curtain windows.
A pot of rattle snake stew
Cooking over a campfire spindle.

Old general bunion he knew
How to sing-a-song or two.

I'm an Okie from Muskogee
And I am in love with you

Michael Thomas

#4
Lust - A Sonnet

Woulds't thou in most gentle manner favor
Overzealous suitors bestirred fanatical.
Hardly knowing thy disposition or manner,
Yet pursuing thee quick and impractical?

Time oft allows hasty hearts, as love oft is:
Less rational, by far, greater irrational.
As emotion guides weaker minds insists
That at their back, death hastens to call.

But warning is offered the wayward soul
The woman led down the path of poetry.
That indenture blurs independence's goal
And beware words that make you hurry.

But, for me, indeed, I throw all that to hell
Bidding you give in to lust's chapel bell.

Miss you sacred spell your grin evoking blue
Inside my anxiousness wanting eyes like yours behind my back
So when I turn,
you will be watching me and hands beneath my chin
Modeling me to wishes of your sensibilities
kissing me gently on the cheek.

After the evening ended,
darkness surrounded me as a midnight church
alone with only an echo of god's grace
in solemn scented odored incense.

I could not find you,
nor was there hope of my sleep without you.
I called to the lonely sand-man
and was forced to withdraw into night.

It might be too late to say how I care for you
as amber clings to its yellow cloak.

I will let you go with no words allowing me relief.
Too soon we find each other.
Too late we want time to stop.

#6

It is last call.
The haves seen through smoky filtered restaurant windows,
warm in candlelight of amber comfort.
The have-not peek into a world of abundance.
Some where there is an end to the gifts of favor.
Outside the magical sense of privacy,
there is a ghost of deprivation waiting to invade the rich.
It is as inevitable as a machine grinding to a purpose.
We sit and beneath the stillness grows
an insistent rumbling of discontent.
I fondle you with measures of my eyes.
I sooth you with words of affection
and blind you to the coming crisis.
We both will be caught in the time of famish.
We will be lined up and shot
and thrown into a ditch of lime covered injustice.
There will be no prayers for the dead,
only a sad silence as the smell rises noxious.
The simple fact of our memory will be blotted out
by time of terror / by time of destitution.
Rain will be our brother washing us bit-by-bit
and erasing all indications of our once life.
Oh! My mother serenade me with your sadness.
Call to me in my sorrow and lift me up to your eyes.
I am a pilgrim of the horror of unkindness.
I am a burden to the light. I am the dark innocence of betrayal
by the obsidian powers of indifference.
Hail to the new order of importance.
Let there be no indication of my once-held affection for you.
Bow to the wrench-of-grunge. Kneel to the sanctimonious
scourge. The air is thin with the smell of blood
and there is no room for white lace
between the curtains of hell holding in the acrid smoke
of bonfires in distances. It is last call.

  Prostrate thyself atop the ashes of envy. It is last call

Hey little cutie
Show me some booty
Some of your tutti-fruity
It's like your bitching duty

Now don't be shy or don't be rude
You a bitch fine beauty not a dude
I'm a nigga got a bigger piece of wuude
Ain't leading you down the wrong ruuoade

Whoa!! Look at that smile on your face
You got something no preaching nun can erase
Gotta good set of rocker knockers in place
I aim to have you home run rounding the base

Every one of them boozer losers straying in the hood
Want to get you to their party but they never could
They flat on their ass coked-out acid brain of wood
You all primp and skimp steady like a whore should

Whoa!!
Take it easy mama I ain't dis you but I miss you good

#8
What I have to offer

This is what I offer while we are alive
Joy overriding sorrow now and after we die
Earth is a complicated planet to survive
And laughter the only remedy when we cry

Across the veil I will comfort you
Help you forget what pain you went through
Give you trust for all you must do
Reincarnating to establish a life that is new

I am not perfect
I am constant
I will waver
And abjure

But I have always given all that I have
And I refuse to change, no matter what

I cannot say love is forever
Only that my heart and soul are

A Sonnet To Love:

Time must hold still for my words to you.
I have willed your heart to listen to mine.
Feel the pulse of excitement of love new.
Together in hope that our spirits entwine.

The danger to wishes is always mistrust.
In faith we are innocent as we hold hope
That fervor and promises are less lust,
And more genuine than quick-to-elope.

Oh! I have a ladder, a hidden scheme,
Two pair underwear, one packet of soup.
A map for the future leads to a dream,
A cell phone, credit card, pouch with a loop.

But I know you want to wait for time to pass
So, I'll read, watch and sleep on the grass.

#10

I am not dainty but a carnivore of blood flesh.
The rabbit and creatures of woodland green
Became the food for my ligaments and veins.

I am not a delicate prince but a beast of everything
Filling my belly with the cooked entrails of my neighbors.

My disposition for cooked meat follows my link to evolution
So close to my time that avoidance is impossible.

I feel the stirrings of inner wholesomeness
I give my soul over to the gift of deer and cow
Resting so lovely inside my psyche and stomach.

Without these nourishment's I would be imbalanced..
With them I am grateful for my health and gratitude.

The memory of the friends resting inside of me
Doubles the lives of us and we become one in joy.

Days of Light

The beleaguered heart
is the heart of caution.

The confident heart
is the heart of venturesome.

We cannot be free of self-indulgence
until we free ourselves from our self-pity.

Color my memories in blood roses
laid upon the bier of my timelessness.

How often we return to the colors of joy
is how we color our remembrances.

Mellow is my soul from having been
pricked by the rose of love.

Into my dreams of her are forty years of happiness
buried beneath the trellis of sanguine mysteries.

Let this flower speak of love's nourishment
fed by the sun of secrets
quieted by the moon of blue.

Love is entwined with the seasons
as flowers follow the days of light.

Michael Thomas

An Unfulfilled Dream

All rights reserved The string ties me to the past
come unraveled from spools
turned brown from time.

The string is too weak
to bring you back to me
or, you were too heavy
from all your promises
that I kept in my
fathers R G Dun
cigar box with the
broken seal.

If I could color you as a child would do
I would go over the lines of your form
with crayons of all the colors you
evoked in me over the years:
Red for excitement blending
into orange sunsets and
orchards of fruit tangled
into a blue clouded sky.

The yellow in your hair
would still blind me
as it spread over
green grass.

Sleep comes easy by the fading blue
spreading itself thin over night's indigo.
Somewhere little sparks of stars
released my eyes into dreams.

Carolyn, small parts of you,
I knock on wood to keep me safe from evil.

I could not avoid your stubbornness of stone endurance.
I only needed to wait out the allotted hours
in which you never returned
and the blues overtaking me.

Waving flags herald my heart of silence
and I lean away from the fires of your passion
like marshmallows on skewer sticks.
Do not call me a fool for enduring the memory
of an unfulfilled dream.

Schubert Lieder Auf dem Wasser Zu Singen, D. 774 – Elly Ameling & Rudolf Jansen

da da da da da daaaaaa da
da da daaaaaa da da da
da da da da da daaaaaa da
da da daaaaaa da da da

the little moments when our hearts do meet
those little moments of such perfect clarity

the little moments when our hearts do meet
I soar above the soft touch of your hand
I sweep over the beauty of your grace

these precious moments when our hearts touch
I cannot hold myself still and I waft into emotion

If life were always like this, I would want to live forever
when your eyes become ambrosia of delicacy
when your fingers lift veils from words of secrecy
the little moments when our hearts become one

da da da da da daaaaaa da
da da daaaaaa da da da

come into this center of stillness

give me your little heart to grow
into a thing of magic and mystery

I love you in these moments when we touch
I cannot love you more than a blind awareness
I love you in Auf dem Wasser zu singen forever
I love you on oceans sung forever

Glen Campbell

I don't remember who I am.
There are no teleprompters here.
I am led along a quiet river bank
by a friend who holds my hand.
It seems the birds sing to the slip of water
making ripples over shallow inclines.

If I could play an instrument
it would be a violin.
Leafs dangle on swaying branches.
The soft buzz of the cicada is strung into the wind.

I have no idea of eating or sleeping.
My friend changes faces.
She says her name is Kimberly
and she talks on-and-on showing me shadows
of Cal, Shannon and Ashley, who she calls "love children".

Occasionally my fingers touch guitar strings.
Often the peaceful melodies somewhere deep inside me
make me want to cry, but I am a big man now and my friend
squeezes my hand leading me along
as I fall in-and-out of so many dreams.

Michael Thomas

My Ex Wife

We married after Vietnam,
   both equally stupid.
After five years of bitterness, I smothered her.
I wrapped her; put her in my car trunk,
   and removed all evidence of her presence in my house.
When I buy a new car, I switch trunks on her.
She gets lighter every year.

Perception

You can feel bad food.
Hear crappy music
from the juvenile's car at the red light.

We all know the secret desires we harbor
to smash our buggies into the jerks in line ahead of us.

I feel really stupid stopping for a funeral line of cars
that snake their way through red lights.
And, I often want to pull in front of a fire truck
just to irritate the fire people going for a joy ride.

When I sit in church on Sunday,
I do not love my neighbor for coughing
without covering their face.
I hate the preacher telling us that we are sinners
just because he has the upper hand with god.

I apologize for being so crabby,
but I do not want to buy-one to get-one free.

If the best and most beautiful things must be felt
then I will go to the museum
and run my hand along all the marble statutes
even if the guard wants to arrest me.

Thank you for listening to my words
because I do not trust your response
but enjoy having confused you for reading
but not understanding.

Round and Round

I come close to insanity.
I never quite step over the line.
I am small potatoes and not noteworthy.
My insignificant life is one of small traumas
that I seem to be able to resolve with no great acclaim.
I solve my own internal quandaries
as a secret internal process
that needs not be divulged to others.

Maybe insanity is being alone.
I may be insane in a quiet private manner.
Being alone is not dark or intensely negative.
I am simply alone with all the wealth of information
that I keep accessible within my conscious capabilities.

I truly love all the information
that I keep crammed inside my thinking process.
Maybe that is insanity:
To love the information that I revolve within me.
Round and round the information goes
and where it stops,
no one knows.

Refrain from the Dance

Buried, no-tell, pith of tree,
Avocado seed, acorn
Kept kernels of thought

We imagine women
Like the cat smells
Curiosity captivates
The dull edge of passion

The knife cuts
The ax splits
We are diced
By desire

The most disappointing
Was being woken sober
And, the night lifts veils
On morning's scales

She sleeps Cinderella
She wakes the witch
 I am never quite sure
What drove me
Into the fires
Of hell
 But it is best said that:
The remedy for romance
Is to refrain from the dance

Michael Thomas

Achilles Awakens

earth has an agenda
core remnants remind the oceans of deserts
without human intervention we have all of nature
from a distant star, the earth is but another ball
encircling the earth
are striations of molecules
grouped together in swirling patterns

these molecules carry genetic information
that permeates energy groups residing within
earth, air, fire and water composites

all habitation, whether it is animal, vegetable or mineral,
receive these molecules at their willful predisposition

so, if a habit-ant of earth, residing within the sphere,
has a level of awareness and engages or limits its awareness
then, the system is dependent upon all habit-
ants level of awareness

In early stages of earth development
evolutionary beginnings
gave early habit-ants
greater awareness

as species increased and developed
on their evolutionary schedules of awareness
then,
complications reduced the spiritual awareness,

overall within the system

and, therefore, nature fills the vacuum
and adjusts the balance on the earth
to correct imbalances

In our meatloaf earth noodle salad
tectonic plates float us to oblivion

from the comfort of our living room
we watch Mauna Loa Mauna Loa
display our insignificance

We have had all of Greek
to warn us of philosophy
overrunning our psyche

We have Rome proving
longevity eventually ends

Achilles sleeps through
end-of-Troy and wakes
to a new beginning

My Indiscretions

I celebrate the friends I've made
and bow to those I've lost.
May there be no flowers fade,
living free life has its cost.

But there upon the foamy brine
a flotsam bark will float
of pieces once that were mine:
of sins and songs I wrote.

Hearts heavy with sorrow
I elevate to my own pardon.
I give no care to tomorrow
And place love in my garden.

Sweet kiss thy furrowed brows,
close myself to all intentions.
Upon the ocean as it growls
soft I wash my indiscretions. Silence

I sing you now of silence
sorrow with no cease.
Give you over license
to do with what you please.

The world falls into pieces
where history makes no sense.
All death and all diseases
carry guilt or penance.

Our wish to be understood
comes with much frustration.
We are animals, bad-or-good,
feeling sadness or elation.

Look to the children of our seed
never back to last tomorrow.
We live with what we need
And pay for what we borrow.

Soft love from all your kisses,
kneeling praying redemptions.
No less than all our wishes,
our heights or declinations.

Listen to the music of our heart
where all our misguided intentions
change by the healing's that impart
in all the melodic dimensions.

Oh! Songs of choral awakening
We're enriched by syncopation.
We fall to sleep ascending
the scales of eternal notation.

Hope

I feel for my blanket
tucked under my chin.

The cat finds a comfortable indentation
satisfied of my affection in the descendant night.

How all things find their way without light
is how the owl sleeps on a branch
as its instincts keep it safe.

I cannot be a worm because I would
want to wake up someday
in the promise of
a sunrise.

Remember there is despair and hope
that exist in yin-and-yang
that exist in love-and-hate
that exist in churchyard shadows
where the lingering ghosts
relax beneath the cover
of a season void of life.

My fingers feel for you
and I sleep in peace
with you close
to me in hope.

My Daughter

It was not love
brought you open.

The hospital neon ceiling blinked.

Everyone watching you emerge,
from the silver glucose afterbirth,
waited for that first cry announcing
Achilles at the trench
bellowing for Patroclus.

It was a quiet sigh of accomplishment
that clocked you into time.

Your mother became empty of you.
She just wanted to fill her womb
with silence and her heart to sleep.

Memorial Day Expose

3,100 BC, Inanna the Sumerian goddess of love, fertility and warfare. She sailed the Euphrates with her lions and soldiers. She scourged the land in battle. The great princess of war bequeathing to us our first written words of poetry adoring this uncouth barbarian.

"From the Great Above Inanna opened her ear to the Great Below" She descended into the underworld accompanied with her faithful servant and adviser Ninshubur.

Ereshkigal, who is Inanna's dead sister, castigates and forces Inanna to accede to the rules of the underworld and brands her warrior sister with shame and stricture.

We, of today, memorialize, not Inanna but all the dead who bled into the land the red soil of our sorrow.

Inanna and Zalmoxis are crucified and come back from the dead to save their peoples in circa 3,100 BC.

1,260 BC, Greek history replete with war and death, records the fall of Troy and the complete destruction of the city that ends the Trojan War.

We, of today, memorialize, not the heroics, but the deaths of civilians and soldiers of this war.

Odysseus sails home to Penelope.

Aeneas deserts Dido and sails from Carthage to found the city of Rome by defeating the Tunis in warfare.

We of today, memorialize, not this history, but the death of all the peoples who left their bones and blood on the grounds surrounding Rome.

753 BC to 476 CE or AD Rome ends and Constantine founds Constantinople.

We, of today, memorialize the Xia dynasty of China and the great list of emperors who scourged the vast lands of the East killing and destroying cities in their wake.

356 BC, Alexander the Great sweeps over all of the land between the Mediterranean Sea and the Indian Ocean.

We, of today, memorialize the millions of dead who shed their lives in battle or in their homes during this time of conquest.

330 to 1453 CE or AD Byzantine Empire of revolts and civil wars such as Anastasian War, Iberian War, Vandalic War, Moorish Wars, Gothic War, Lazic War, etc.

We, of today, memorialize this trail of dusty dead souls that meld into the earth their bodies.

Each successive century running through the Crusades leads us to the end of the Byzantine period of history.

1593 Battle of Sisak
1624 Siege of Breda
1692 Action at La Hogue
1712 Battle of Denain
1745 Battle of Fontenoy
1779-1783 Great Siege of Gibraltar
1800 Battle of Marengo
1805 Napoleon at the Battle of Austerlitz
1868 The Sea Battle of Lissa
1916 Battle of the Somme
1937 Battle of Belchite
1941-1945 World War II
1953 East German Uprising
1956 Hungarian Revolution
2009 Chechen Wars

We, of today, memorialize the passed-on peoples who laid to rest beneath the rubble of so many wars and revolutions.
We pray for the chirping of the morning birds
Listen intently to the cooing of the doves in solitude
Across the split of horizons simple in their silence, we listen to the earth spin
To our ancestors we hand them our cell phones and pray for their reunion with us
Amen, we say at the end of our services
Alleluia, we sing for peace
And we sleep with all our doubts
Arriving

what does it take to console
that dark mist of unknown
lying within these hours
that collect like dust
beneath counter tops
in hidden spaces
where thoughts
avoid going
it takes bravery to accept
a self-security of forever

a sparse soul knows
neither greater or lessor
makes no difference to peace

only the ocean keeps its secrets
only the forests hide the lichen and moss
inside the canopy of slow and silent trees

being secure within ourselves
means we endure to be there when others need us

never will suicide do
it is an ultimate escape
that will double back upon us

here are the stars within our grasp
the little moons of midnight reflection

this intact black space holding each console of galaxies
within its power

I fall to affection for the distance
neither measurable nor understandable
I give in to the magic of prophecy that each sun
 teaches us in patience
I have always been here
arriving is an afterthought
of being comfortable
with each moment
of existence

Sega Boom

Sir Alex adjusted his visor shield
and re-aimed the periscope to advantage.
"There are three hot spots
popping up around the edge of that structure to the left".
"Sir Alex, we do not have rounds that can reach them"
Andromeda put her hand on Sir Alex's shoulder.
Sir Alex became quiet and waited.
Somewhere inside her helmet,
Andromeda heard the words coming from a distance:
"You are not a child anymore. This exercise is real.
This is no longer a game. You are a soldier now".

The T-29 tank was rumbling in neutral.
Andromeda motioned to the driver to pull forward.
There was a crunch of gravel as the tank tracks swiveled
and pulled the monster tank into the deserted street.
A fusillade of akak tracers lit up the scene like Christmas lights.

Sir Alex crowded low behind the tank with Andromeda at his side.
The tank turret exploded with successive rounds
tearing the side of the structure into bits of scattered pieces.
Andromeda yelled to Sir Alex, "Have the hot spots gone away?"

Sir Alex thought only of one thing: Wait for the dust to clear.
Wait for the dust. He had learned that hot spots become active
quickly after the dust settled. Wait for the dust.
He waived his hand in a swirling motion
so that Andromeda recognized his meaning,
to wait for the dust to thin.

When a few minutes had passed
and the scene became clearer,
both Sir Alex and Andromeda saw the three bodies lying
beneath the fallen building bricks.
The enemy were dead and the tank inched forward
without opposition.

Smooth Edge of a Saw

in all fairness, look to the chumps who fly erratically
under the radar they make lots of money
and buy expensive homes needing cleaning crews

Amanda mops and vacuums once a week
Philip keeps the boiler room operating
I remember one chump who felt no qualms
in violating agreements
the reason for his brashness:
"I am a lawyer. Let them try to out-sue me"
we litigate
we do not hesitate
he who does ain't a councilor

money is a funny thing
it is only as good as what you do with it

people always want more
they have no idea of what to buy
other than to satisfy their shallowness

there never was one person
who took their money with them after death
the only thing we take with us, across the veil, is our soul
if someone lived correctly and added kindness to their soul,
then that kindness is their resume

I have no idea which end of a pliers to use
the smooth edge of a saw cuts slower

here is my aunt Minnie
she eats but she's not skinny
her cabinets are full of food
it puts her in a good mood
my aunt Minnie lost her husband in the war
and she never remarried
because it was too much trouble

Michael Thomas

Why Wednesday?

wars are fought seven days a week
years after years
from country after country
and ages upon ages

seven days a week warriors fight and rest to re-enter the fray

monday they are fresh
tuesday they are in the thick of things
thursday they count their gains or losses
friday thru sunday they heal
but, wednesday, is the day sandwiched between the seven

wednesday is a day warriors cannot pronounce the w-e-d-n
they say - "we wend our way into battle with stout spear and shield"

they say - "praise the lord and pass the ammunition"

they say - wash on monday / iron on tuesday / mend on wednesday / churn on thursday / clean on friday / bake on saturday / rest on sunday

warriors do not iron anymore. They are too busy doing all the other days of the week. Besides, everything for the warrior is synthetic materials and "wash & wear"

warriors fight for victory

but remember, there are the defeated warriors who go back home to their wives and children and families empty handed and without acclimation

these defeated warriors take their place with all the many millions of second rate actors who get shot or killed by the victorious

the studios in heaven, call them "bit part" actors in the big picture

I tried being a warrior once

I left my job at the library filing books, and reading avariciously
I joined the football team and exercised and prepared to be a warrior
when the moment came for the first scrimmage game,
I was placed on defense

My schoolmates ran their first two plays over my position
and flattened me to the ground
I left the field immediately and went back the
 un-heroic job of filing books again

The warrior is best viewed all days of the week
but for wednesay they rest out of the limelight

Warriors never marry on wednesday
They never make major decisions on this day of the week

On wednesday the warrior sits at the bar nursing a
"bump and a beer"

I am Nothing but Glorified in Magnificence

The lord and all his followers
follow behind me in protection.
There were times when I feared
but I turned and felt safe.
There upon the hillocks,
hidden beneath tree boughs,
little birds sang out with bravery
against the seasons changes,
with no fear of how they eat,
they sang in the voice of joy.

How can I blink for danger
when I hear the birds and
I take their message to heart.
I woke with my enemies near.
I clothed myself in the words
of the savior and my enemies
passed around me invisible.
Take what you may of time
and the turning of the seasons,
I am taken into a timeless sleep
where "watcher" guards protect me.

The airless paths of darkness
become lighted by the graces.
The noisy pieces of human indifference
drift into silence with my Lord whispering
of how I am loved and needed in eternity.
I am like a wary creature beneath a sky
where the twist of a twig or the sound of wind
alert me to the guides who follow me.

I am nothing but glorified in magnificence
by the acceptance of my heart within the
sacredness of Jesus, Buddha and Mohammad.

Author's Biography:

Writer, philosopher, philanthropist Michael Thomas is a long- time CPA from Canton, Michigan and a fine poet. We "discovered" him languishing in an online poetry site, writing who knows what to who knows whom. To our great satisfaction, he has taken to publishing his words, and the world is all the richer for it. Here he is doing an impersonation of a Detroit Mafia Hitman.

Also by Michael Thomas

ISBN: 978-1500192037

ISBN: 978-1492297567

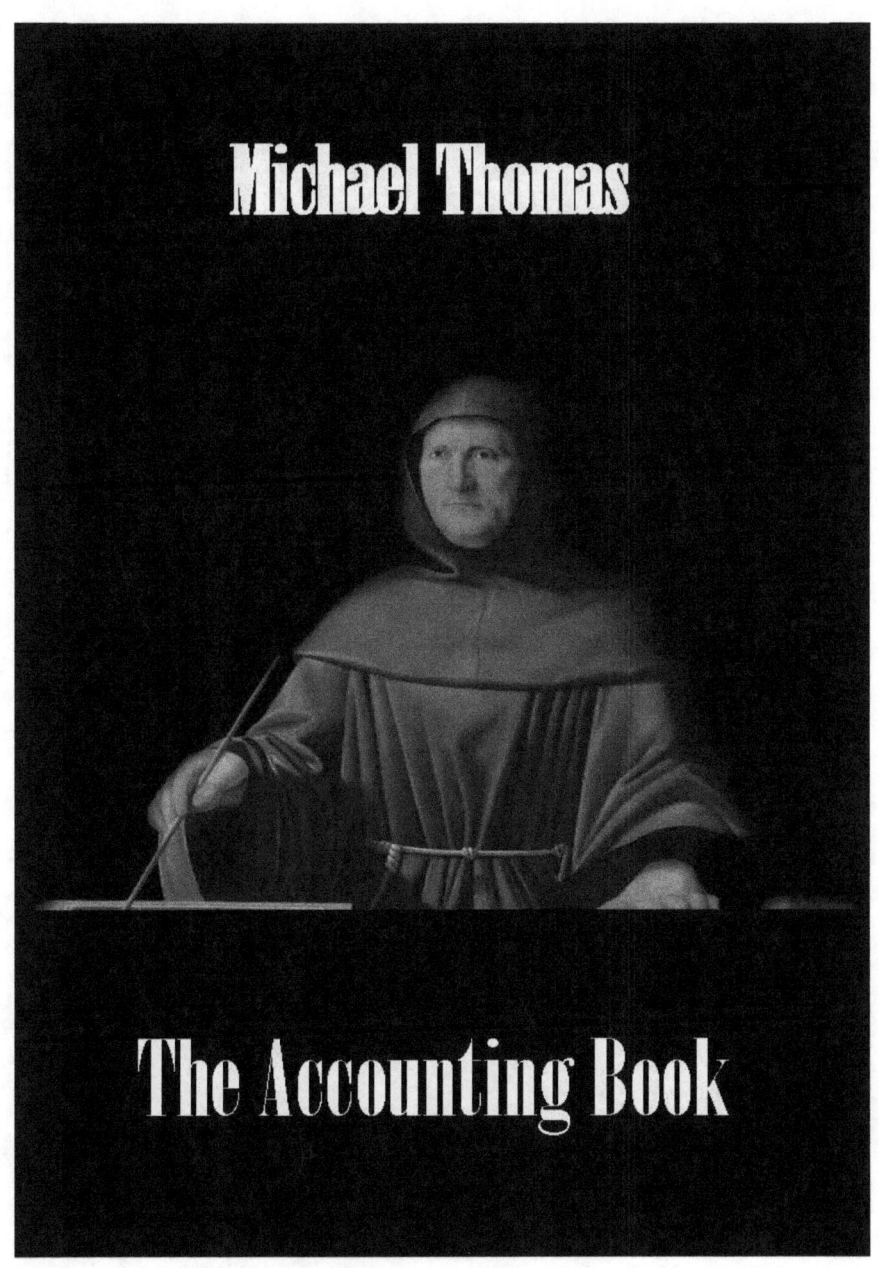

ISBN: 978-1500267889

ISBN: 978-1492776932

ISBN: 978-1495419010

ISBN-13: 978-1501063275

Michael Thomas Poetry
Volume 4

ISBN: 978-1507634387

Michael Thomas Poetry Volume 5

ISBN: 978-1514174104

ISBN-13: 978-1329825413

These and other books by independent authors
can be found at:

www.shoestringbookpublishing.com

Shoestring Book Publishing offers
simple and affordable quality book publishing.

The <u>smart</u> choice
for the <u>wise</u> independent authors voice!

Send your inquiry today to: Shoestringpublishing4u@gmail.com
Contact Allan 207-922-8837
or Alison 732-331-7863

Please Review!

All independent authors depend upon reviews left on Amazon.com by readers to help promote their books. Without these reviews, they will hardly get any notice. Please take the time to leave a short review. Simply go to Amazon.com, find the book and go to the book's page. Under the author's name will be a list of reviews and stars. Click here and there will be a big button saying "Create your own review". Please click here and review.

It only takes a minute!

www.ingramcontent.com/pod-product-compliance
Lightning Source LLC
LaVergne TN
LVHW051044080426
835508LV00019B/1691